Medical Ethics

Other books in the Current Controversies series:

Medical Ethics

Laura K. Egendorf, *Book Editor*

Bruce Glassman, *Vice President*
Bonnie Szumski, *Publisher*
Helen Cothran, *Managing Editor*

CURRENT CONTROVERSIES

GREENHAVEN PRESS
An imprint of Thomson Gale, a part of The Thomson Corporation

Detroit • New York • San Francisco • San Diego • New Haven, Conn.
Waterville, Maine • London • Munich

LIBRARY OF CONGRESS CATALOGING-IN-PUBLICATION DATA

Medical ethics / Laura K. Egendorf, book editor.
    p. cm. — (Current controversies)
Includes bibliographical references and index.
ISBN 0-7377-2212-6 (lib. : alk. paper) — ISBN 0-7377-2213-4 (pbk. : alk. paper)
    1. Medical ethics. I. Egendorf, Laura K., 1973– . II. Series.
R724.M29273 2005
174.2—dc22   2004060566

Printed in the United States of America

Contents

Chapter 2: What Ethics Should Guide Organ Transplants?

Foreword

By definition, controversies are "discussions of questions in which opposing opinions clash" (Webster's Twentieth Century Dictionary Unabridged). Few would deny that controversies are a pervasive part of the human condition and exist on virtually every level of human enterprise. Controversies transpire between individuals and among groups, within nations and between nations. Controversies supply the grist necessary for progress by providing challenges and challengers to the status quo. They also create atmospheres where strife and warfare can flourish. A world without controversies would be a peaceful world; but it also would be, by and large, static and prosaic.

The Series' Purpose

The purpose of the Current Controversies series is to explore many of the social, political, and economic controversies dominating the national and international scenes today. Titles selected for inclusion in the series are highly focused and specific. For example, from the larger category of criminal justice, Current Controversies deals with specific topics such as police brutality, gun control, white collar crime, and others. The debates in Current Controversies also are presented in a useful, timeless fashion. Articles and book excerpts included in each title are selected if they contribute valuable, long-range ideas to the overall debate. And wherever possible, current information is enhanced with historical documents and other relevant materials. Thus, while individual titles are current in focus, every effort is made to ensure that they will not become quickly outdated. Books in the Current Controversies series will remain important resources for librarians, teachers, and students for many years.

In addition to keeping the titles focused and specific, great care is taken in the editorial format of each book in the series. Book introductions and chapter prefaces are offered to provide background material for readers. Chapters are organized around several key questions that are answered with diverse opinions representing all points on the political spectrum. Materials in each chapter include opinions in which authors clearly disagree as well as alternative opinions in which authors may agree on a broader issue but disagree on the possible solutions. In this way, the content of each volume in Current Controversies mirrors the mosaic of opinions encountered in society. Readers will quickly realize that there are many viable answers to these complex issues. By questioning each author's conclusions, students and casual readers can begin to develop the critical thinking skills so important to evaluating opinionated material.

Current Controversies is also ideal for controlled research. Each anthology in the series is composed of primary sources taken from a wide gamut of informational categories including periodicals, newspapers, books, United States and foreign government documents, and the publications of private and public organizations. Readers will find factual support for reports, debates, and research papers covering all areas of important issues. In addition, an annotated table of contents, an index, a book and periodical bibliography, and a list of organizations to contact are included in each book to expedite further research.

Perhaps more than ever before in history, people are confronted with diverse and contradictory information. During the Persian Gulf War, for example, the public was not only treated to minute-to-minute coverage of the war, it was also inundated with critiques of the coverage and countless analyses of the factors motivating U.S. involvement. Being able to sort through the plethora of opinions accompanying today's major issues, and to draw one's own conclusions, can be a complicated and frustrating struggle. It is the editors' hope that Current Controversies will help readers with this struggle.

"Chinese medical ethics has developed over several thousand years and many feel that its teachings, which emphasize care and respect for patients, are worth incorporating into Western ethics."

Introduction

Like nearly all professions, the medical industry has unscrupulous practitioners. However, most doctors, whether in Western or Eastern nations, adhere to basic codes of ethics. For doctors who have been trained in the Western tradition, the two most important codes are the Hippocratic Oath—including its modern version—and Thomas Percival's *Code of Medical Ethics*. The Greek doctor Hippocrates developed the first code in the fifth century B.C. The traditional text asks doctors to make this vow:

> I will prescribe regimens for the good of my patients according to my ability and my judgement and never do harm to anyone. To please no one will I prescribe a deadly drug nor give advice which may cause his death. Nor will I give a woman a pessary [suppository] to procure abortion. But I will preserve the purity of my life and my art. I will not cut for stone, even for patients in whom the disease is manifest; I will leave this operation to be performed by practitioners, specialists in this art. In every house where I come I will enter only for the good of my patients, keeping myself far from all intentional ill-doing and all seduction and especially from the pleasures of love with women or with men, be they free or slaves.

This oath has of course changed somewhat in modern times; for example, many doctors perform abortions, and the medical treatment of slaves is not an issue in modern Western medicine. An updated version of the oath was written in 1964 by the academic dean of the school of medicine at Tufts University and is used in many medical schools. Doctors who take the revised oath vow to be understanding and sympathetic toward their patients, to seek the assistance of their colleagues, and to "remember that I do not treat a fever chart, a cancerous growth, but a sick human being."

In between the ancient Hippocratic Oath and its modern reworking, the most significant contribution to Western medical ethics was made by the English physician Thomas Percival. His *Code of Medical Ethics*, published in 1803, lists the duties required of doctors, such as evaluating the conduct of their fellow health care professionals and not allowing the use of inferior drugs.

The Western interpretation of medical ethics is not the only kind in use today. Chinese medical ethics has developed over several thousand years and many feel that its teachings, which emphasize care and respect for patients, are worth incorporating into Western ethics, especially as Eastern medicine becomes more common in the West.

According to Guo Zhaojiang, a professor in China's Fourth Military Medical University, Chinese medical professionals must follow six basic rules: use all means available to help the dying and wounded; practice medicine with honesty; constantly work on improving medical skills; behave politely; treat all patients equally; and do not be arrogant or disrespectful of other people's achievements. As he explains in the *Journal of Medical Ethics*, "Influenced by the excellent Confucian thinking and culture, a rather highly-developed system of Chinese traditional medical ethics emerged with a well-defined basic content, and the system has been followed and amended by medical professionals of all generations throughout Chinese history."

Chinese medical ethics actually predate the Confucian era. Two key publications marked the emergence of Chinese ethical teachings. First, Bian Que, a fifth-century B.C. physician sought to eliminate the dangers posed by sorcery—a then-common method of curing ailments—by developing ethical guidelines. Second, the medical text *Yellow Emperor's Canon of Internal Medicine* declared that medical workers must possess a noble moral character. Still, it was the Chinese philosopher Confucius (c. 551–479 B.C.) whose teachings, which emphasized ethics, helped form the underpinnings for medical ethics in that nation. His works did not appear until after his death—his teachings were written down by his disciples—but Confucius's lessons in morality have affected the Chinese from his generation and beyond.

At their core Confucian medical ethics are about love and benevolence—doctors show love for their patients by healing them. Doctors further exhibit these noble feelings by neither disrespecting nor causing harm to their patients and by treating patients equally regardless of wealth or social status. This equality of treatment was important in a nation that in the centuries surrounding Confucius's life was in a constant state of war and political upheaval. The continual changes in the structure of Chinese society made it more difficult for people to determine how to treat one another. By following the precepts set by Confucius, the Chinese—be they doctors or otherwise—were provided with a consistent way to interact. Furthermore, as Daqing Zhang, the associate chair of the Peking University Center for History of Medicine in Beijing, China, and Zhifan Cheng, the center's chairman, explain in an article in the *Hastings Center Report*, the Confucian code of ethics was intended to ensure that doctors acted virtuously. They write, "In [Confucianists'] eyes, conscience was the foundation of medical virtue, doctors should have a sense of pity, of shame, of respect, and of right and wrong."

In more recent years, however, Chinese medical ethics have moved away from a strict Confucian interpretation. Chinese doctors are now influenced by Western medical practices. For example, the development of hospitals means that doctors are no longer responsible only to their patients—who had always been the foremost concern under traditional Chinese medical ethics—but also to their hospital and colleagues. Furthermore, emerging medical technology in fields such as reproduction has brought about new ethical questions.

Just as Chinese doctors are gradually influenced by Western ethics, so too are Western doctors learning from the teachings of Confucius. In many ways these two versions of medical ethics are not so different; the well-being of the patients is of primary concern. The growing popularity of "alternative" treatments common to China—notably, acupuncture and herbal remedies—in Western nations shows the intertwining of Western and Eastern medicine and suggests that the two ethical traditions can be combined to the benefit of patients. As David E. Guinn, the executive director of the International Human Rights Law Institute, contends in an article in the journal *Second Opinion*, incorporating non-Western ethics into conventional Western medicine is beneficial. He writes, "[Eastern] values are not, for the most part, antagonistic to the values of conventional medicine. They supplement them. They hint not only at the limitations of current healthcare ethics, but also at how current norms may be expanded to embrace a more holistic, integrated model of care."

Whether they are Western or Eastern in origin, medical ethics are an essential element of health care. Patients cannot be sure they will receive adequate care if they have doubts that their doctors and health care providers will treat them with respect. In *Current Controversies: Medical Ethics*, the authors evaluate the fairness of the health care system, the ethical questions surrounding organ transplants, the ethics of reproductive technology, and the morality of genetic technologies. No matter the time or place in which they developed, medical ethics help set forth the rules of one of life's most basic relationships: that between doctor and patient.

Chapter 1

Is the Health Care System Fair?

Chapter Preface

One of the primary criticisms of the U.S. health care system is that disadvantaged groups, such as minorities and the poor, receive inadequate medical care due to bias and a lack of resources. Many commentators contend that a segment of the American populace that is at particular risk of exploitation is the disabled. The belief held by many people that the life of a disabled person is not one that is worth living suggests to numerous analysts that the health care system is not entirely fair or ethical.

Assisted suicide is a particular concern of disability rights advocates. They fear that disabled people are often viewed as unable to experience satisfying lives and may be pressured into ending their lives. Medical ethicist Wesley J. Smith, in his book *Culture of Death*, argues, "Disabled people are especially worried about using quality of life as a yardstick of moral worth." He adds that modern American society has been unwilling to provide disabled people with help that will improve their lives, such as personal assistants.

Concerns about assisted suicide are not unfounded. The case of Tracy Latimer, a twelve-year-old Canadian girl with severe cerebral palsy who was euthanized by her father, has been used by disability rights advocates to show how the disabled are often treated unethically. Although this case occurred in Canada, it has much to teach Americans crafting health care policies, many contend.

Robert Latimer killed his daughter via carbon monoxide poisoning. At the time of her death, Tracy weighed forty pounds and had the cognitive abilities of a three-month-old baby. She was unable to walk, talk, or feed herself, was reportedly in constant pain, and had undergone numerous surgeries. Robert Latimer was convicted of second degree murder, which in Canada carries a minimum sentence of ten years, although the judge in the case unsuccessfully sought to reduce Latimer's sentence to less than two years. The jury had suggested that Latimer be eligible for parole after one year.

Advocates of the disabled were aghast not only at Tracy Latimer's death but at the desire of the judge and jury to lessen her father's sentence. They argued that such actions only further prove that the lives of the disabled are viewed as worth less than those of their able-bodied peers. Furthermore, the girl's murder was seen as the cruel and callous act of a man who did not wish to be inconvenienced by his ill daughter and who ignored any signs of her humanity. Mark Pickup, a Canadian advocate for the disabled, wrote in the *Human Life Review*, "Misery and pain were not the sum total of Tracy Latimer's life any more than misery and pain are the sum total of the lives of countless other people with severe disabilities. Tracy was a happy child. . . . Tracy's father put her out of *his*

15

misery." Pickup also criticizes Tracy's mother, who sided with the defense, and the media for exaggerating the woes of Tracy's life.

The murder of Tracy Latimer is an extreme case, but it suggests that certain vulnerable populations such as the disabled are not considered worthy of full participation in the health care system. The authors in the following chapter debate whether the health care system is fair.

Racial Bias Is Not a Problem in the Health Care System

by Sally Satel

About the author: *Sally Satel is a resident scholar at the American Enterprise Institute.*

One evening in 1994 Dr. Pius K. Kamau was on call at his Denver hospital when a nineteen-year-old car crash victim was admitted to the intensive-care unit coughing up blood. The young man, a white supremacist skinhead sporting a swastika tattoo, was shocked to look up from his bed and see Kamau, a black man, taking care of him. The patient refused to have anything to do with his doctor. "He never talked to me directly; all of our dealings were via white nurses," Kamau writes. "They interpreted to him what I said, as if I spoke in another language. He never allowed his open eyes to rest on mine again."

Despite the difficulties, Kamau did his work and the patient recovered. The doctor had fulfilled the Hippocratic ideal to which he was sworn: being an honorable agent of the patient. Judging from the searching personal essay he wrote about the experience, I think Kamau would be deeply offended at the suggestion that a physician might compromise his standard of care for patients such as this hate-filled nineteen-year-old.

The Conventional Wisdom

According to new conventional wisdom, however, it takes far less than an insufferably bigoted patient to cause a physician to lower his standard of treatment. A mismatch in race between doctor and patient—especially when the doctor is white and the patient is not—may be enough to trigger subtle, or not so subtle, biases that result in second-rate medical treatment and poorer health. "It is increasingly evident that African-Americans and other minority patients have strong grounds for doubting both the goodwill and the color blindness of white medical practitioners," writes Kenneth DeVille of the Department of Medical Humanities at the East Carolina University School of Medicine. No less authoritative a voice than the American Medical Association's official newspaper has claimed that "a growing body of research reports that racial disparities in health status can be explained, at least in part, by racism and discrimination within the health care system itself." This is why, according to the Reverend Al Sharpton, health will be the "new civil rights battlefront," a prediction echoed by other black leaders, including the Reverend Jesse Jackson, National Association for the Advancement of Colored People [NAACP] chairman Julian Bond and the Congressional Black Caucus.

In a 1998 radio address delivered during Black History Month, President Clinton spoke of race and health. "Nowhere are the divisions of race and ethnicity more sharply drawn than in the health of our people." It is indeed true that black Americans are less healthy than whites and Asians on a number of measures, such as life expectancy, infant mortality and death from cancer. This often remains true even when insurance coverage is taken into account. Beyond these facts, the president could only speculate when he said that perhaps one of the reasons for racial disparities is "discrimination in the delivery of health services."

Bias in the Past

Given the history of systematic racial discrimination and segregation in the health care system, lingering bias seems, at first, plausible. Black patients were treated on separate and inferior hospital wards—a policy that persisted at many hospitals in the Deep South until the late 1960s. Once routinely barred from joining hospital staffs and medical societies, black physicians started their own institutions to treat other blacks who were denied adequate care by the white-controlled medical facilities. As late as the mid-1960s several medical schools had restrictions against admitting black students.

A particularly appalling episode in medical research was the Tuskegee Syphilis Study, whose purpose was to study the natural progression of the disease in black men. In the notorious "experiment," which lasted from 1932 to 1972, roughly four hundred black men in the late stages of syphilis were never told of their condition, never given any kind of treatment and never warned about transmitting it—grossly unethical practices that would never be tolerated today.

Decades later, however, accusations of medical bias still linger. According to Vanessa Northington Gamble, a physician and vice president of Community and Minority Programs at the Association of American Medical Colleges, "Tuskegee symbolizes for many African-Americans the racism that pervades American institutions, including the medical profession." In the fall of 1999 the U.S. Commission on Civil Rights informed Congress and the White House that "racism continue[s] to infect" the health care system. Earlier that year an official of the Association of American Medical Colleges commented on physicians' unwitting biases. "Most doctors think they are fair," he told the *Boston Globe*. "That they carry bias is very hard for them to think about."

Why Disparities Exist

For her part, Leslie Pickering Francis, a medical ethicist at the University of Utah, prefers to believe that "racism [is] the presumptive cause of . . . health care problems minorities face" until there is evidence to the contrary. This view is increasingly common—not too surprising considering the habit nowadays of presuming that discrimination inevitably lies beneath the surface of any race-related difference in social outcome. But evidence suggests that many race-related differences in health are not what they seem to observers like Professor Francis, Reverend Sharpton and the Commission on Civil Rights.

The charge of physician bias against minority patients is often made reflexively, overlooking the myriad complicated reasons for differences in care. In this [viewpoint] I present evidence that supports other interpretations of "health disparities," as they are often called. . . .

Less eye-catching than accusations of bias are the everyday aspects of clinical care that account for many of the recorded disparities. For example, one reason procedure rates differ is that medical problems do not necessarily occur with the same frequency across races. As a 1999 report from the Henry J. Kaiser Family Foundation points out, "It should be noted that every differential in care is not necessarily a problem and the level of care obtained by whites may not be the appropriate standard for comparison." Consider these facts: uterine fibroid tumors, and thus hysterectomies, are more common in black women than in whites, while osteoporosis-related fractures, and thus hip replacements, are rarer. Limb amputation is more common among black patients, typically because thicker atherosclerosis of the blood vessels in the leg makes it harder to perform limb-saving surgery.

> *"The charge of physician bias against minority patients is often made reflexively, overlooking the myriad complicated reasons for differences in care."*

African Americans suffer stroke at many times the rate of whites yet undergo a procedure to unclog arteries in the neck (endarterectomy) only one-fourth as often. Racism? Unlikely. Some studies have documented a greater aversion to surgery and other invasive procedures among African American patients, but the more substantial reason, in the case of endarterectomy, is clinical. It turns out that whites tend to have their obstructions in the large, superficial carotid arteries of the neck region, which are readily accessible to surgery. Blacks, by comparison, tend to have their blockages in the branches of the carotids. These smaller vessels run deeper and further up into the head where the surgeon cannot reach them.

Thus, even without financial obstacles, an African American patient at high risk for stroke is far less likely than a white counterpart to undergo endarterectomy. Yet indoctrinologists like David R. Williams, a sociologist at the University of Michigan's Institute for Social Research, are quick to turn this disparity into evidence of bias. After all, they argue, if money is not an issue, then the difference in treatment *must* represent bias on the part of the doctors. *American Medical News,* the newspaper of the American Medical Association, gives voice to this view: "National studies, such as one that examined care at Dept. of Veterans Affairs medical facilities—where all of the patients have comparable insurance coverage—suggest 'racial disparities in the quality of medical care do not merely reflect the behavior of a few bad apples,' Dr. Williams said. 'The evidence is too overwhelming and the pattern is too pervasive.'"

Williams seems not to consider a different interpretation: the patients' clinical needs rather than the doctors' personal biases are dictating the care. Think about it: If not for concern about the patient (many of whom are treated in private hospitals and have health insurance), why wouldn't physicians perform a reimbursable procedure?

The Hospital Effect

Another consideration in performing procedures is the clinical condition of the patient. Does he have other medical problems that alter the risk-to-benefit ratio of a procedure and make the outcome less favorable? The treatment of heart disease, for example, often needs to be modified in the presence of uncontrolled high blood pressure and diabetes—conditions more typical of black patients with heart disease than of their white counterparts.

Then there is the site of care itself. Some hospitals simply do not offer certain cardiac procedures, such as bypass grafts or balloon angioplasty. Examining a sample taken from New York City hospitals, Dr. Lucian L. Leape of the Harvard School of Public Health and his colleagues found that about one-fifth of all patients needing these procedures do not get them, largely because those hospitals do not offer them. Leape found that failure to recommend these procedures—and hence to transfer a patient to a hospital where it could be performed—is equal across all groups of black, white and Hispanic patients. Conversely, when medical care is readily available for special patient populations (for example, the veterans' affairs medical centers or the military services), racial differences in treatment and outcome can melt away. For example, veterans with colorectal and prostate cancer show no race-related differences in treatment availability, treatment methods or survival rates. . . .

The racial disparities in health are real, but data do not point convincingly to systematic racial bias as a determinant.

Rationing Health Care Can Be Ethical

by Edmund D. Pellegrino

About the author: *Edmund D. Pellegrino is a professor emeritus of medicine and medical ethics at the Center for Bioethics at Georgetown University Medical Center.*

Dr. Kohler has covered a lot of ground in his essay[1]—the state of our nation's health care system, the success and problems of the Oregon Health Care initiative, and the ethical issues associated with rationing. Each deserves serious consideration, but I will confine myself to his ethical questions for two reasons; first, the moral question is, I believe, central to any attempt to fashion a just health care system; and, second, Dr. Kohler misconstrues my position on the ethics of rationing.

When all is said and done, I agree with Dr. Kohler that *explicit* rationing can be morally justified. It is definitively not excluded by my assertion that health care is a moral obligation of a good society. Indeed, it is only through recognition of that moral obligation that explicit rationing is justified. Let me begin with definitions—at least those that define the argument as I see it.

Defining Rationing

Rationing I take to be a conscious, planned allotment of resources of a particular good in accordance with some principle or criterion of distribution. Rationing is *per se*, therefore, neither good nor bad morally. Its moral status is determined by the reasons for which the process is undertaken, the justification of the criteria for distribution, and the priorities and degrees of fairness that govern the process of allotment.

De facto rationing is not rationing, strictly speaking. Rather, it is fortuitous,

1. This viewpoint was published in response to an essay by Peter O. Kohler that also appeared in the summer 2002 edition of *Pharos*.

unplanned and the result of the interplay of accidental sociopolitical, geographic, and economic factors. *De facto* rationing takes on a moral tone when we became aware of its existence, and fail to remedy the conditions that bring it about. The existence of *de facto* rationing is not therefore a justification for rationing, as too many proponents of rationing assume.

Both genuine rationing and *de facto* rationing involve the question of distributive justice, that is, the principle and virtue of a good society that aims to provide for each citizen what is his or her due. Distributive justice is more than fairness, which focuses on a just method of distribution of a scarce resource. The process of distribution must itself be judged by a more fundamental principle of justice.

Managed care, like rationing, is, *per se*, a morally neutral concept. Its moral status also depends upon its aim, the means it uses to attain that end, and the priorities it follows in the allotment of health care resources. Thus, both managed care and rationing may have good ends and purposes like quality of care, a just distribution of resources, correction of imbalances of distribution, and the like. Or they can have profit as the motive, cost containment, allotment by ability to pay alone. Or they may depend on pitting physician self-interest against the patient's interests by bonuses, preferments for denying care, and so on. The purpose, means, and priorities must each be assessed ethically and not by exigency alone.

When Rationing Is Justified

Against this background I would respond to Dr. Kohler's question "Is explicit rationing ever justified?" as follows:

Yes, explicit rationing can be morally justified if certain conditions are met. Dr. Kohler cites a few of my conditions. I will expand that list a bit.

First of all, there must indeed be a crisis—a present or foreseeable situation in which health care expenditures threaten to compromise other societal goods that a good society is under obligation to provide: education, national defense, public safety, and protection of human rights.

Second, other effective measures such as efficiency, productivity, and optimization in the use of resources must have been exhausted. The size, expense, and enormous paperwork, and the administrative burdens of the present system must be eliminated.

> *"Explicit rationing can be morally justified if certain conditions are met."*

Third, the full array of expenditures of a society, particularly discretionary expenditures in the private and public arena must be examined critically. This is essential because so many insist that we cannot afford universal coverage. Americans should be asked to examine how their enormous expenditures for amusement, gambling, alcohol, tobacco, and illicit drugs can be justified when millions of Americans are uncovered, or covered inadequately, against illness, disease, and disability.

Some would say these are "one-time" savings and therefore not part of a permanent solution. This may be so, but they have yet to be tried in any systematic way. If these preliminary measures have been instituted and these conditions satisfactorily met, then rationing, that is, "explicit distribution of absolutely scarce, beneficial resources" (to use Dr. Kohler's phrase) is morally justified. Indeed, it is morally mandatory if we agree that health care is a good owed by a good society to its members.

A Clear and Explicit Process

Attention then must be turned to the process of rationing which must also meet certain criteria of ethical propriety. For one thing, the process must indeed be explicit, as Dr. Kohler suggests. The criteria for distribution and the process itself should be guided by societal mechanisms and *not* left implicit—that is, determined by the clinician at the bedside. The clinician must be free to protect the interest of his patient, and to seek within the system that which his patient needs. This may require some sacrifice of self-interest.

The clinician cannot therefore be the rationer. Even when rationing is morally justified in the name of distributive justice, the physician must remain the guardian of commutative justice—that is, of what is due to individual sick persons as a consequence of the nature of the physician-patient relationship. In implicit rationing—rationing carried out by the physician—the physician is forced to act against his own patient's needs. He becomes an adversary, not an advocate.

The criteria for rationing must be publicly known and transparent. They must be arrived at by some mechanism that allows for societal input. This is the promise behind the Oregon plan[2] described by Dr. Kohler, as well as the inclusion of more of the uncovered population. Whether this has been achieved, and to what degree in the Oregon plan, is not the subject of my comments. Legitimate questions have been raised about the fairness of the process, its bureaucratic structures, rising costs, and sources of funding. However these things are eventually judged, the ethical requirement of public participation is a strength of the plan.

Most crucial for ethical rationing is a clear exposition of the criteria of distribution—whether by disease category, severity of need, ability to pay, age, societal merit, or equity. The justice implications of each of these criteria make up a significant proportion of the ethical concerns felt by many about the Oregon plan.

In the end, the decisions to ration health care—when it is justified, what criteria of distribution are chosen, how the process is conducted, and the role of the clinician and his method of payment—will reveal the kind of society we Ameri-

2. Oregon's health plan, an attempt to provide health care coverage to everyone in the state, was implemented in 1994. Its goal has not yet been achieved.

cans want to have and be. We have had debate about medical and health care for much of the last century, most of it focused on fine tuning what we have, emphasizing cost containment, and predicting economic catastrophes if access to care is universalized.

An Ethical Debate

The central moral issue has not been engaged. Do the sick, ill, disabled, and infirm have a moral claim on our society for alleviation of pain and suffering? Is there a societal obligation to relieve human suffering? Is it a concern of a good society to assure that there is a just and fair distribution of the means modern medicine affords for relief? Is medical and health care a universal human need, a good so important to human flourishing that a good society owes it in justice to its citizens?

This is where the debate should start. If the answers to these questions are affirmative, then rationing can be addressed and used in an ethically defensible way according to the criteria outlined above. Rationing is not the issue. Nor is it managed care. Both must be judged by ethical criteria. How those criteria are justified will be the measure of the kind of society we choose to be.

In short, the whole debate should be ethically driven. It must start with recognition of societal obligation, and then proceed to ethically defensible measures of organization, distribution, and ministration to human needs. Continued dissatisfaction with managed care and coverage are indication enough that as a nation we are unhappy with our choices. Yet we lack the courage to confront the ethical issue. Only then can political and economic mechanisms be chosen with any degree of rationality. What the outcome will look like we cannot predict. What is clear is that an ethically driven health care system will look different than what we have today.

Dr. Kohler has raised the right question. How shall we answer as a society?

Legalizing Physician-Assisted Suicide Does Not Lead to Abuses

by Peter Rogatz

About the author: *Peter Rogatz is a doctor and a founding board member of Compassion in Dying of New York and a former professor at the State University of New York at Stony Brook.*

Every reasonable person prefers that no patient ever contemplate suicide—with or without assistance—and recent improvements in pain management have begun to reduce the number of patients seeking such assistance. However, there are some patients who experience terrible suffering that can't be relieved by any of the therapeutic or palliative techniques medicine and nursing have to offer, and some of those patients desperately seek deliverance.

Physician-assisted suicide isn't about physicians becoming killers. It's about patients whose suffering we can't relieve and about not turning away from them when they ask for help. Will there be physicians who feel they can't do this? Of course, and they shouldn't be obliged to. But if other physicians consider it merciful to help such patients by merely writing a prescription, it is unreasonable to place them in jeopardy of criminal prosecution, loss of license, or other penalty for doing so.

Two Important Principles

Many arguments are put forward for maintaining the prohibition against physician-assisted suicide, but I believe they are outweighed by two fundamental principles that support ending the prohibition: patient autonomy—the right to control one's own body—and the physician's duty to relieve suffering.

Society recognizes the competent patient's right to autonomy—to decide what will or won't be done to his or her body. There is almost universal agreement that a competent adult has the right to self-determination, including the right to have life-sustaining treatment withheld or withdrawn. Suicide, once illegal throughout the United States, is no longer illegal in any part of the country. Yet assisting a person to take her or his own life is prohibited in every state but Oregon. If patients seek such help, it is cruel to leave them to fend for themselves, weighing options that are both traumatic and uncertain, when humane assistance could be made available.

The physician's obligations are many but, when cure is impossible and palliation has failed to achieve its objectives, there is always a residual obligation to relieve suffering. Ultimately, if the physician has exhausted all reasonable palliative measures, it is the patient—and only the patient—who can judge whether death is harmful or a good to be sought. Marcia Angell, former executive editor of the *New England Journal of Medicine*, has put it this way:

> The highest ethical imperative of doctors should be to provide care in whatever way best serves patients' interests, in accord with each patient's wishes, not with a theoretical commitment to preserve life no matter what the cost in suffering. . . . The greatest harm we can do is to consign a desperate patient to unbearable suffering—or force the patient to seek out a stranger like Dr. Kevorkian.[1]

Refuting the Arguments Against Assisted Suicide

Let's examine the key arguments made against physician-assisted suicide. First, much weight is placed on the Hippocratic injunction to do no harm. It has been asserted that sanctioning physician-assisted suicide "would give doctors a license to kill," and physicians who accede to such requests have been branded by some as murderers. This is both illogical and inflammatory. Withdrawal of life-sustaining treatment—for example, disconnecting a ventilator at a patient's request—is accepted by society, yet this requires a more definitive act by a physician than prescribing a medication that a patient has requested and is free to take or not, as he or she sees fit. Why should the latter be perceived as doing harm when the former is not? Rather than characterizing this as "killing," we should see it as bringing the dying process to a merciful end. The physician who complies with a plea for final release from a patient facing death under unbearable conditions is doing good, not harm, and her or his actions are entirely consonant with the Hippocratic tradition.

Second, it is argued that requests for assisted suicide come largely from patients who haven't received adequate pain control or who are clinically depressed and haven't been properly diagnosed or treated. There is no question that proper management of such conditions would significantly reduce the number of patients who consider suicide; any sanctioning of assistance should be contingent upon prior management of pain and depression.

---

1. During the 1990s Michigan doctor Jack Kevorkian assisted in more than 130 suicides. He was convicted of murder in 1999 and sentenced to ten to twenty-five years in prison.

However, treatable pain is not the only reason, or even the most common reason, why patients seek to end their lives. Severe body wasting, intractable vomiting, urinary and bowel incontinence, immobility, and total dependence are recognized as more important than pain in the desire for hastened death. There is a growing awareness that loss of dignity and of those attributes that we associate particularly with being human are the factors that most commonly reduce patients to a state of unrelieved misery and desperation.

Third, it is argued that permitting physician-assisted suicide would undermine the sense of trust that patients have in their doctors. This is curious reasoning; patients are not lying in bed wondering if their physicians are going to kill them—and permitting assisted suicide shouldn't create such fears, since the act of administering a fatal dose would be solely within the control of the patient. Rather than undermining a patient's trust, I would expect the legalization of physician-assisted suicide to enhance that trust. I have spoken with a great many people who feel that they would like to be able to trust their physicians to provide such help in the event of unrelieved suffering—and making that possible would give such patients a greater sense of security. Furthermore, some patients have taken their own lives at a relatively early stage of terminal illness precisely because they feared that progressively increasing disability, without anyone to assist them, would rob them of this option at a later time when they were truly desperate. A patient contemplating suicide would be much less likely to take such a step if he or she were confident of receiving assistance in the future if so desired.

Fourth, it is argued that patients don't need assistance to commit suicide; they can manage it all by themselves. This seems both callous and unrealistic. Are patients to shoot themselves, jump from a window, starve themselves to death, or rig a pipe to the car exhaust? All of these methods have been used by patients in the final stages of desperation, but it is a hideous experience for both patient and survivors. Even patients who can't contemplate such traumatic acts and instead manage to hoard a supply of lethal drugs may be too weak to complete the process without help and therefore face a high risk of failure, with dreadful consequences for themselves and their families.

> *"It seems improbable that assisted suicide would pose a special danger to the elderly, infirm, and disabled."*

Fifth, it is argued that requests for assisted suicide are not frequent enough to warrant changing the law. Interestingly, some physicians say they have rarely, if ever, received such requests, while others say they have often received requests. This is a curious discrepancy, but I think it can be explained: the patient who seeks help with suicide will cautiously test a physician's receptivity to the idea and simply won't approach a physician who is unreceptive. Thus, there are two subsets of physicians in this situation: those who are open to the idea of assisted suicide and those who aren't. Patients are likely to seek help from the former but not from the latter.

Frequent Requests for Assistance

A study carried out a few years ago by the University of Washington School of Medicine queried 828 physicians (a 25 percent sample of primary care physicians and all physicians in selected medical subspecialties) with a response rate of 57 percent. Of these respondents, 12 percent reported receiving one or more explicit requests for assisted suicide, and one-fourth of the patients requesting such assistance received prescriptions.

A survey of physicians in San Francisco treating AIDS patients brought responses from half, and 53 percent of those respondents reported helping patients take their own lives by prescribing lethal doses of narcotics. Clearly, requests for assisted suicide can't be dismissed as rare occurrences. Sixth, it is argued that sanctioning assisted suicide would fail to address the needs of patients who are incompetent. This is obviously true, since proposals for legalization specify that assistance be given only to a patient who is competent and who requests it. However, in essence, this argument says that, because we can't establish a procedure that will deal with every patient, we won't make assisted suicide available to any patient. What logic! Imagine the outcry if that logic were applied to a procedure such as organ transplantation, which has benefited so many people in this country.

Avoiding the Slippery Slope

Seventh, it is argued that once we open the door to physician-assisted suicide we will find ourselves on a slippery slope leading to coercion and involuntary euthanasia of vulnerable patients. Why so? We have learned to grapple with many slippery slopes in medicine—such as Do Not Resuscitate (DNR) orders and the withdrawal of life support. We don't deal with those slippery slopes by prohibition but, rather, by adopting reasonable ground rules and setting appropriate limits.

The slippery slope argument discounts the real harm of failing to respond to the pleas of real people and considers only the potential harm that might be done to others at some future time and place. As in the case of other slippery slopes, theoretical future harm can be mitigated by establishing appropriate criteria that would have to be met before a patient could receive assistance. Such criteria have been outlined frequently. Stated briefly, they include:

1. The patient must have an incurable condition causing severe, unrelenting suffering.
2. The patient must understand his or her condition and prognosis, which must be verified by an independent second opinion.
3. All reasonable palliative measures must have been presented to and considered by the patient.

4. The patient must clearly and repeatedly request assistance in dying.

5. A psychiatric consultation must be held to establish if the patient is suffering from a treatable depression.

6. The prescribing physician, absent a close preexisting relationship (which would be ideal), must get to know the patient well enough to understand the reasons for her or his request.

7. No physician should be expected to violate his or her own basic values. A physician who is unwilling to assist the patient should facilitate transfer to another physician who would be prepared to do so.

8. All of the foregoing must be clearly documented.

Application of the above criteria would substantially reduce the risk of abuse but couldn't guarantee that abuse would never occur. We must recognize, however, that abuses occur today—in part because we tolerate covert action that is subject to no safeguards at all. A more open process would, in the words of philosopher and ethicist Margaret Battin, prod us to develop much stronger protections for the kinds of choices about death we already make in what are often quite casual, cavalier ways."

> *"The humanitarian benefits of legalizing physician-assisted suicide outweigh [the risk of abuse.]"*

It seems improbable that assisted suicide would pose a special danger to the elderly, infirm, and disabled. To paraphrase John Maynard Keynes, in the long run we are all elderly, infirm, or disabled and, since society well knows this, serious attention would surely be given to adequate protections against abuse. It isn't my intention to dispose glibly of the fear that society would view vulnerable patients as a liability and would manipulate them to end their lives prematurely. Of course, this concern must be respected, but the risk can be minimized by applying the criteria listed above. Furthermore, this argument assumes that termination of life is invariably an evil against which we must protect vulnerable patients who are poor or otherwise lacking in societal support. But, by definition, we are speaking of patients who desperately wish final release from unrelieved suffering, and poor and vulnerable patients are least able to secure aid in dying if they want it. The well-to-do patient may, with some effort and some good luck, find a physician who is willing to provide covert help; the poor and disenfranchised rarely have access.

The Dutch and Oregon Experiences

Eighth, it is argued that the Netherlands experience proves that societal tolerance of physician-assisted suicide leads to serious abuse. Aside from the fact that the data are subject to varying interpretation depending upon which analysis one believes, the situation in the Netherlands holds few lessons for us, because for many years that country followed the ambiguous practice of technically prohibiting but tacitly permitting assisted suicide and euthanasia.

The climate in the United States is different; our regulatory mechanisms would be different—much stricter, of course—and we should expect different outcomes. The experience of Oregon—the only one of our fifty states to permit physician-assisted suicide—is instructive. During the first three years that Oregon's law has been in effect, seventy terminally ill patients took advantage of the opportunity to self-administer medication to end protracted dying. Despite dire warnings, there was no precipitous rush by Oregonians to embrace assisted suicide. The poor and the uninsured weren't victimized; almost all of these seventy patients had health insurance, most were on hospice care, and most were people with at least some college education. There were no untoward complications. The Oregon experience is far more relevant for the United States than the Dutch experience, and it vindicates those who, despite extremely vocal opposition, advocated for the legislation.

Do Not Punish Patients

Ninth, it has been argued that a society that doesn't assure all its citizens the right to basic health care and protect them against catastrophic health costs has no business considering physician-assisted suicide. I find this an astonishing argument. It says to every patient who seeks ultimate relief from severe suffering that his or her case won't be considered until all of us are assured basic health care and financial protection. These are certainly proper goals for any decent society, but they won't be attained in the United States until it becomes a more generous and responsible nation—and that day seems to be far off. Patients seeking deliverance from unrelieved suffering shouldn't be held hostage pending hoped-for future developments that are not even visible on the distant horizon.

Finally, it is argued that the status quo is acceptable—that a patient who is determined to end his or her life can find a sympathetic physician who will provide the necessary prescription and that physicians are virtually never prosecuted for such acts. There are at least four reasons to reject the status quo. First, it forces patients and physicians to undertake a clandestine conspiracy to violate the law, thus compromising the integrity of patient, physician, and family. Second, such secret compacts, by their very nature, are subject to faulty implementation with a high risk of failure and consequent tragedy for both patient and family. Third, the assumption that a determined patient can find a sympathetic physician applies, at best, to middle- and upper-income persons who have ongoing relationships with their physicians; the poor, as I've already noted, rarely have such an opportunity. Fourth, covert action places a physician in danger of criminal prosecution or loss of license and, although such penalties are assumed to be unlikely, that risk certainly inhibits some physicians from doing what they believe is proper to help their patients.

I believe that removing the prohibition against physician assistance, rather than opening the flood gates to ill-advised suicides, is likely to reduce the incentive for suicide: patients who fear great suffering in the final stages of illness would have the assurance that help would be available if needed and they would be more inclined to test their own abilities to withstand the trials that lie ahead. Life is the most precious gift of all, and no sane person wants to part with it, but there are some circumstances where life has lost its value. A competent person who has thoughtfully considered his or her own situation and finds that unrelieved suffering outweighs the value of continued life shouldn't have to starve to death or find other drastic and violent solutions when more merciful means exist. Those physicians who wish to fulfill what they perceive to be their humane responsibilities to their patients shouldn't be forced by legislative prohibition into covert actions.

There is no risk-free solution to these very sensitive problems. However, I believe that reasonable protections can be put in place that will minimize the risk of abuse and that the humanitarian benefits of legalizing physician-assisted suicide outweigh that risk. All physicians are bound by the injunction to do no harm, but we must recognize that harm may result not only from the commission of a wrongful act but also from the omission of an act of mercy. While not every physician will feel comfortable offering help in these tragic situations, many believe it is right to do so and our society should not criminalize such humanitarian acts.

America's Class Structure Has Created an Unfair Health Care System

by Vicente Navarro

About the author: *Vicente Navarro is a professor of public policy, sociology, and policy studies at the Johns Hopkins School of Public Health and the editor in chief of the* International Journal of Health Services.

Editor's Note: This viewpoint was originally given as a speech at a seminar at Johns Hopkins University in 2003.

The health sector of the United States is in profound disarray. Even though the United States spends more on health care (14 percent of its GNP [gross national product]) than any other country, we still have problems that no other developed capitalist country faces. Let me list some of them. The first and most overwhelming problem is that no less than forty-four million of our people have no form of health benefits coverage whatsoever. The majority of them are working people, and their children, who cannot afford to pay the health insurance premium that would enable them to get care in time of need. Many of them work for small companies that cannot or will not pay their part of the health insurance premium. Because these individuals cannot pay for insurance, they do not get needed care, and many die as a consequence. The most credible estimate of the number of people in the United States who have died because of lack of medical care was provided by a study carried out by Professors David Himmelstein and Steffie Woolhandler. They concluded that almost 100,000 people died in the United States each year because of lack of needed care—three times the number of people who died of AIDs. It is important to note here that while the media express concern about AIDs, they remain almost silent on the topic of deaths due to lack of medical care. Any decent person should be outraged by this situation. How can we call the United States a civilized nation when it denies the basic human right of access to medical care in time of need? No other major capitalist country faces such a horrendous situation.

Inadequate Insurance

But the problem does not end here, with the uninsured. An even larger problem is the underinsured, that is, people whose health benefits coverage is inadequate. Most people find, at a crucial moment in their lives when they really need care, that their health insurance coverage does not include the type of medical problem they have, the type of intervention they need, or the type of tests or pharmaceuticals they require—or, that it covers only a minute portion of what must be paid for the services. We, as Americans, are the citizens with the least amount of health benefits coverage in the western world. Even the federal programs, such as Medicare (which in theory should cover all care for the elderly), are very insufficient. In every European country and in Canada, the elderly do not

> *"Racism and sexism have an enormous influence on the health conditions of people living in the United States."*

have to pay for the pharmaceuticals they need. Not so in the United States, where many elderly must cut back on necessities in order to pay for the drugs they need. In the United States, 35 percent of the elderly cut back on their food purchases so they can afford their medications. But where the cruelty of the system reaches its utmost is among those who are dying. Among the terminally ill, 39 percent indicate that they have "moderate to severe problems" in paying their medical bills. No other major capitalist country comes even close to this level of inhumanity.

The overwhelming majority of people living in the United States are faced with such inhuman prospects due to inadequate health care. You may have seen the movie *John Q*, which shows the anger and frustration of a manufacturing worker who suddenly finds out (as do millions of Americans every day) that treatment of his son's life-threatening condition is not covered by the family's health insurance.

Obviously, the problem in the United States is not lack of funds. As I mentioned before, we spend much more on health care than any other country. What, then, is the cause of this situation?

Class Structure in the United States

In order to answer this question, we have to understand how power is distributed in the United States. Indeed, the health care sector of any society is the best mirror of the power relations existing in that country. In the United States, most people would agree that race is a category of power. In general, whites have more power than blacks or Hispanics. And the mortality statistics reflect this. A black man with a cardiovascular disease is 1.8 times more likely to die of it than is a white man with the same disease.

Also, it is generally agreed that men have more power than women. Gender and race are indeed categories of power. But these factors by themselves cannot explain why we have the type of health services we have. Needless to say, racism and sexism have an enormous influence on the health conditions of people living in the United States and on the characteristics of the country's medical care sector. But, they alone do not go to the root of the problem, which is *class power.* The most important variable that predicts people's type of work, education, housing, consumption, and standard of living, and the types of diseases they have and how long they are likely to live, is the class they belong to. Of course, within each class, race and gender play a significant role. But in today's United States, class is the most important category of power. A blue-collar worker with cardiovascular disease is 2.4 times more likely to die of the disease than is a corporate lawyer. Class mortality differentials are, indeed, the largest mortality differentials in the United States.

I am aware that class is almost an un-American category. It is widely assumed in the media that we are a middle-class society, with the majority of our people in the middle, a few at the top—the rich—and a few at the bottom—the poor. This is the most commonly referred to class structure in the United States: rich, middle class, and poor. Also, in polls people are frequently asked to define themselves by the group to which they belong. *Time* magazine regularly asks people, are you upper class, middle class, or lower class? Not surprisingly, most people respond "middle class." Actually, I have always admired the tolerance and patience of average folks. I must admit that if someone were to ask me whether I am a member of the lower class, I would respond "your mother also!" "Lower class" is clearly an offensive term. Yet large sectors of our working people are frequently referred to as the lower classes. Classism is as prevalent in the language as are racism and sexism, if not more so.

This perception of our class structure—rich, middle, poor, or upper, middle, lower—is heavily ideological and profoundly wrong. Actually, our class structure is remarkably similar to that of most of the capitalist developed countries of Europe. At the top we have a group that in Europe is called the bourgeoisie. We don't use that term since it sounds too French. We call this group the corporate class, since most of its members are the top brass of corporate America. These are the individuals whose incomes derive primarily from property. It includes, among others, top executives of insurance companies and the [chief executive officers] CEOs of large corporations—groups that play a key role in the health care sector of this country.

> *"Class mortality differentials are . . . the largest mortality differentials in the United States."*

Next we have what Europeans call the petit bourgeoisies, but what we call the upper-middle classes, which include owners of mid-size enterprises and highly trained and paid professionals, among others. Below this, in terms of power, is the middle class, which includes craft workers and artisans, self-employed people, and technical and administrative personnel. Then we have the working class, which includes clerical, manufacturing, and service workers, individuals who are supervised, who work at repetitive jobs, and are paid by hourly wages. The working class represents around 60 percent of our population—the majority of the U.S. population.

Work-Related Health Benefits

How does class power explain the U.S. health sector? Very easily. The United States is alone among the developed capitalist countries in not having a national health program, a universal health care program funded by the government or by social security. The United States is also the only country in the developed world where most people get their health benefits coverage through their employer. This unique situation is rooted in the Taft-Hartley Act, which basically legislated that the working people of this country should have their health benefits coverage through highly decentralized collective bargaining agreements. This explains why the steelworkers in Baltimore, who have strong unions, have fairly comprehensive health benefits coverage, while the clerks in the local supermarket, who don't have a union, have pretty lousy health benefits coverage or no coverage at all. Let me point out, though, that even those sectors with the best coverage, like the steelworkers, have much less coverage than their fellow workers in all other developed capitalist countries. Moreover, in the United States, even these workers are losing their coverage in today's anti-union climate. Today steelworkers pay 32 percent of all their medical care costs as out-of-pocket expenses, a 50 percent increase over just five years ago. The deterioration of the economic situation is having an enormous human cost. More than one million people (mostly workers and their families) lose their health insurance every year, and another sixty-two million see their health benefits coverage reduced or their premiums increased.

Notice, too, that if your health insurance benefit is dependent on your job, then when you are fired, you lose not only your salary but also the health benefits coverage for yourself and your family. This is why workers think twice before making trouble, since getting fired has a higher human cost in the United States than in any other country. And this was precisely the intention of the Taft-Hartley Act: to discipline labor. The employers knew the value of work-related health benefits as an instrument to discipline labor. The Taft-Hartley Act also forbids the working class of the United States to act as a class. It forbids sympathy strikes, which is why steelworkers cannot strike in support of, for example, coal miners. This inability to go out on sympathy strikes weakens labor dramatically. Again, no other country has this type of legislation. Not even

Prime Minister [Margaret] Thatcher was able to put such a law, as she intended to, through the British Parliament. If the working class could add pressure as a class (as do workers in other countries when they call a general strike to make their voice heard), then it could have enormous power, certainly enough to force the government to provide health benefits through progressive taxation.

You may well ask why this situation continues and is reproduced. The answer is, again, because of *class power*, that is, because the corporate class, such as insurance bosses and large employers, has enormous power in our political system. This class power manifests itself in many different forms. One of them is the class composition of the top decision-making bodies of our government: 84 percent of cabinet members, 78 percent of the Senate, and 62 percent of the House over the last forty-two years have been members of the corporate class. The remainder have been members of the upper-middle class. There are very few from the lower-middle class or from the working class. One of these is a senator for Maryland, Barbara Mikulski, who was a social worker before being elected to the U.S. Senate. Politicians of working class backgrounds tend to be the most progressive. But there are remarkably few of them in the U.S. Congress.

The Working Class Lacks Decision-Making Power

Let me stress that the same class composition we see in these decision-making bodies of our government also occurs in our health care institutions. For one example, look at who sits on the Board of Trustees of the Johns Hopkins University and of the Johns Hopkins Hospital. You will see that they are the CEOs of some of the most powerful insurance, banking, and manufacturing corporations in Maryland. Actually, there is not one hospital in the entire Baltimore region that has on its board a member of the working class—which happens to be the majority of the Baltimore population.

These points need to be made, because in our country you may have been encouraged to check for the presence of minorities and women in positions of power, and to denounce institutions as discriminatory when you see very few minorities and women in them. I encourage you to continue doing this. But I have to stress that if your concern is—as it should be—to improve the representativeness of our institutions, then class plays a key role. You should ask not only about the race and gender of the members of boards, but also about what class they belong to, pressing for changes in the class composition of those boards. If you press for that, you will soon encounter an enormous resistance—much, much larger than when you ask for an end to race or gender discrimination.

"The United States is alone among the developed capitalist countries in not having a national health program."

Another way that class power is reproduced in our political system is through the privatization of the electoral process. Here again, we in the United States are quite unique. In no other country does money play such a key role in the electoral process. As Senator Mikulski said recently, "money is the milk of politics." And most of that money comes from the corporate class: in 2000, 92 percent of the soft money that went to the key members of Congress who make decisions about health care and financial matters came from large insurance, banking, and employers associations, hospital corporations, pharmaceutical firms, and professional associations, such as the AMA [American Medical Association]. Indeed, it is an alliance of corporate and upper-middle-class interests that pays for those politicians, paying with the aim—successfully achieved—of defending their corporate and professional interests. The profits of the medically related industries, such as the health insurance industries, have reached an all-time high during the administration of George W. Bush, the most class-conscious U.S. president since Hoover.

What Progressives Need to Do

Let me stress here that this situation is often reproduced in the way progressive forces choose to operate. Indeed, we have the most divided progressive community in the developed capitalist world. We tend to focus on gender or on race or on age, or on specific groups or issues. The United States is indeed the country of social movements. I of course applaud this diversity, but it is dramatically insufficient. For example, the United States has a very powerful association of the elderly—the AARP—but our elderly are less taken care of than those in any other developed capitalist country. They don't even have their medications included in their health benefits. We see the same with women. We have a very strong women's association, NOW [National Organization for Women]. But American women have very limited maternity leave: just four weeks without pay. Sweden, which does not have a very strong women's organization, provides a year's maternity leave *with* pay.

Why this difference? Class power is the explanation. If you establish a spectrum of capitalist countries, listing them from very "corporate friendly" (like the United States) to very "worker friendly" (like Sweden), you will find, where the capitalist class is very strong, very poor health benefits coverage (in the public as well as in the private sectors), highly unequal coverage, and very poor health indicators. This is, indeed, the U.S. case. But in countries where the working class is very strong, with a strong labor movement (as in Sweden, which has been governed by a labor party for forty-eight years since the end of the Second World War), you will find very comprehensive health benefits coverage, a more equal distribution of resources, and better health indicators. The lesson here is clear: it is important that we help to strengthen the labor movement in the United States, and in doing so we should also capitalize on the diversity of the social movements, helping those movements to see the basic commonality of their struggles to unite rather than divide working people. This is, indeed, the best thing you can do to improve the health of our people.

Rationing Health Care Is Unethical

by Kip Sullivan

About the author: *Kip Sullivan is a Minneapolis-based writer who writes frequently on health care policy.*

Rationing has long been a dirty word in the health care reform debate. HMOs [health maintenance organizations] hotly deny that they are engaged in rationing. Politicians decry rationing, whether it is inflicted directly by HMOs or indirectly by lack of insurance. Polls consistently indicate that a large majority of Americans oppose rationing as a means to reduce health care spending.

The Rationing Argument

The call for rationing first became audible in the late 1980s as health care inflation worsened. It got louder in the early 1990s as universal health insurance rose to the top of the nation's agenda. It has grown louder still over the last five years as it has dawned on pundits that HMOs are incapable of reining in health care inflation. Here are some examples of statements advocating medical rationing:

• "Eliminating inefficiencies in the system can provide brief fiscal relief, but rationing of beneficial services, even to the well-insured, offers the only prospect for sustained reduction in the growth of health care spending" (Henry Aaron, a prominent economist with Brookings Institution, in a 1990 article for *Science*)

• "Successful cost control will require rationing of services to the very ill" (Aaron, again in a 1992 article for *Health Affairs*)

• "A country can provide unlimited care to a portion of the population or limited care to everyone. But it can't provide everyone with unlimited care, because the demand for health services knows no end" (Jane Bryant Quinn in a 1993 column in the *St. Paul Pioneer Press*)

• "[P]olitical leaders must tell the public the truth . . . : We can't afford unlimited health care. Rationed care is inevitable" (Stephen L. Cohen, a syndicated columnist in a 1999 column for *USA Today*)

• "The question is . . . not if we ration—but how" (David Broder in a 1999 column for the *Washington Post*)

• "No one dares discuss rationing, the most toxic but inevitable of all subjects," (investment banker and government-waste guru Peter G. Peterson in a 2000 op-ed for the *New York Times*)

• *Why It's Time for Health Care Rationing* (a book published by MIT Press in 2000)

Painful Decisions

To give you some idea of how painful a deliberate debate about rationing will be, consider this exercise developed by American Health Decisions (AHD), a nonprofit that, according to its web site, "helps people understand health care choices." AHD conducted focus group sessions in which subjects were asked to state how they would spend $360,000 on the following 6 categories of patients, each of which would cost $120,000 to treat: 4 second-stage cancer patients, 2 heart patients, 2 elderly hip-replacement patients, 1 elderly kidney patient, 1 schizophrenic child, and 4 adults blinded accidentally. (Oddly, the cancer and heart patients were described as "with children.")

You see the problem: These six categories of patients would cost $720,000 to treat, but in this cruel, pretend world you've been asked to play in, you only have $360,000 to spend. Who gets thrown off the island? And by what rationale? Can we cross the three elderly patients (the hip-replacement and kidney patients) off our list and put the schizophrenic child on the must-save list on the basis of age? If you're into pitting kids against the elderly, why not add the cancer and heart patients to the must-save list because they have kids to raise, whereas the four blind adults don't have kids and the elderly patients, if they had kids, have already raised their kids? This implies that you think elderly people are dispensable.

If those choices are not painful and baffling enough for you, consider this choice actually posed to the citizens of Oregon in the late 1980s: Should Oregon's Medicaid program pay for 34 organ transplants for poor people or should it pay for prenatal care and delivery services for 1,500 poor pregnant women? This was how the choice was initially framed for Oregonians in 1987 after Colby Howard, a seven-year-old Oregon boy, contracted leukemia a few months after the Oregon legislature discontinued Medicaid coverage for organ transplants. Had Colby been diagnosed a few months earlier, Oregon's Medicaid program would have paid for the bone marrow transplant that might have saved his life. Colby's mother had managed to raise $80,000 of the $100,000 deposit required by the hospital when Colby died. In the furor that followed Colby's highly publicized death, rationing advocates argued that saving Colby would have meant short-changing other poor people.

Unnecessary and Unethical

But are the rationing advocates correct? Is it true that the only way to insure all Americans is to ration "beneficial services," as Aaron put it? No, it is not. Those who call for rationing now are wrong and unethical. It is unethical for "experts" and "ethicists" to call for medical rationing before we have had a debate about the wastefulness of the U.S. health care system. It is unethical to tell the public that our only choice is one that pits Colby Howard's bone marrow transplant against the medical needs of 1,500 pregnant women, when in fact we could debate many other choices, such as Colby's transplant versus a tiny sliver of the U.S. drug industry's obscene profits (those profits are four times those of the Fortune 500). Or we could debate prenatal services for 1,500 women versus paying the annual salary of one or two HMO lobbyists. Or we could debate treating the two heart patients presented in the AHD exercise versus a half-dozen HMO advertisements.

Rationing, defined to mean the denial of medical services that benefit patients, is rational and ethical only under circumstances in which resources are clearly limited. For example, it makes sense for medics on a battlefield to engage in triage, that is, to treat first those soldiers who are alive but seriously wounded because they stand to benefit more from treatment than those soldiers who are dying or are less seriously wounded. Here's another example: Because only 5,000 livers become available in America each year while 7,000 Americans suffer liver-failure annually, it makes sense for doctors to give liver transplants to the 5,000 patients who will benefit the most.

But it is ludicrous to claim that resources are scarce in the U.S. health care system. The U.S. system, which gobbled up $1.2 trillion in 1999, is grossly inefficient. Experts on both the left and the right share this assessment. Here is an excerpt from a 1989 article in the *New England Journal of Medicine* by Alain Enthoven, a conservative Stanford economist and one of the nation's best-known proponents of a market solution to the health care crisis: "The present system is wasteful in many respects. . . . Much care appears to be of unproved value. There is considerable duplication and excess capacity in our medical facilities. . . . We have a system which is neither efficient nor fair." Here is a comment taken from the front cover of the July 1992 *Consumer Reports*, a magazine that has endorsed a single-payer system: "This year we will throw away at least $200-billion [almost a fourth of total U.S. spending in 1992] on overpriced, useless, even harmful treatments, and on a bloated bureaucracy."

> *"It is ludicrous to claim that resources are scarce in the U.S. health care system."*

By my calculations, the U.S. health care system may be wasting up to $300 to $400 billion dollars a year. To put this in context, it would cost about $30 billion to cover the nation's 43 million uninsured with typical insurance, and perhaps $40 billion to cover the uninsured with insurance that has no deductibles or co-payments.

The waste in the U.S. system may be sorted into five categories: (1) unnecessary services, (2) excessive administrative spending, (3) excess capacity, (4) excessive prices, and (5) fraud. Research on the last three categories is sparse and much of the research on the first two categories (unnecessary services and excessive overhead) was done in the early 1990s when the nation was engaged in a debate about which health care reform proposals would best address the inefficiency of the nation's health care system. Needless to say, these shortcomings in the research mean that a precise estimate of the wasted expenditures is impossible to derive.

Wasteful Spending

But you don't need a precise estimate of the total waste in order to accept the argument that it is unethical to ask Americans to debate rationing before we've debated whether the waste in the system is acceptable. You need only know that the evidence in support of the assertion that the U.S. system is wasteful is compelling. A conservative estimate of the cost of excessive administration spending and excessive prices alone comes to 15 percent of total health spending.

Excessive administrative spending refers both to the administrative spending of insurers and medical providers (doctors, hospitals, etc.). Twenty-five percent of the one trillion dollars we spend on health care each year is spent on administering the system. No one claims that it is possible or desirable to reduce administrative spending to zero. The issue is whether we could spend less than a fourth of our health care dollar on clerks, HMO doctor police, ad writers, lobbyists, merger specialists, and a host of other functionaries who do not provide health care to patients. The evidence suggests that we could cut the share of our health care dollar going to administration down to 10 to 15 percent. In other words, we're wasting $100 to $150 billion annually in administrative costs alone.

> *"It is unethical to ask Americans to debate rationing before we've debated whether the waste in the system is acceptable."*

Several studies indicate that administrative spending grew rapidly as managed care spread. Because HMOs hire people to supervise doctors and hospitals, and because doctors and hospitals hire people to deal with HMOs, this should surprise no one. In a 1996 article in the *American Journal of Public Health*, David Himmelstein and two Harvard colleagues demonstrated that employment of all administrative personnel (that is, administrators in both the insurance and the provider sector) grew by 288 percent between 1968 and 1993 while the number of physicians grew by just 77 percent. A 1996 paper published in *Health Affairs* reported that between 1980 and 1993 hospitals increased their administrative staff by 47 percent (while cutting their nursing staffs by 7 percent). In Minnesota, a state that, along with California, deserves the title of "the cradle of managed care," HMO administrative expenditures rose 403 percent between 1980 and 1991 (the years in which HMOs took over Minnesota's system) while HMO expenditures on medical services rose 255 percent.

Studies that attempt to measure excessive administrative spending by insurers (as opposed to providers) typically compare private-sector U.S. insurers to Medicare or to the national systems of other countries, notably, Canada. Medicare's overhead is 2 to 3 percent while the overhead of private-sector insurance companies ranges from 15 to 30 percent. If you give Medicare a dollar in taxes, Medicare will keep 2 or 3 cents to pay the salaries of its staff, its utility bills etc., and will pay out 97 to 98 cents to doctors. But if you give a dollar in premiums to an insurance company, it will keep 15 to 30 cents for overhead and pay out 70 to 85 cents for medical services. The overhead costs of Canada's "single payer" system are about 1 percent—even lower than Medicare's (probably because Congress requires Medicare to contract with private insurers to process Medicare claims).

Overhead Must Be Reduced

It is not hard to see why Medicare and Canadian health care administrative expenditures are so low. Unlike Aetna or Blue Cross Blue Shield, Medicare and Canada pay little or nothing for marketing, quarreling with doctors about how they should practice medicine, underwriting (which means doing research on a patient's health history and setting premiums accordingly), wining and dining state and federal legislators, paying high salaries to executives, and paying dividends to stockholders.

Now let's switch the subject from insurer overhead to provider overhead. The studies that have attempted to measure excess administrative spending by providers have compared U.S. physicians and hospitals to Canadian physicians and hospitals. In 1991, when single-payer legislation was still on the Congressional agenda, the General Accounting Office published a report on the administrative savings the U.S. could enjoy if its administrative costs (for both insurers and providers) were as low as those of Ontario, Canada's largest province. The GAO found that U.S. providers would enjoy administrative savings equal to 4.5 percent of total health care spending, primarily because billing for physicians is so much easier when they have to bill just one insurer rather than dozens or hundreds, each with different forms and different hoops to jump through.

So if we could reduce insurer overhead to the levels of Medicare or the Canadian system, and if we could reduce provider overhead to the levels of the Canadian system, how much could we save? In the same study in which it analyzed the differences between U.S. and Canadian provider overhead, the GAO also reported that total savings on administrative costs at the insurer level would equal 4.5 percent of total spending. In other words, the GAO concluded that total savings to the U.S. in administrative savings alone from switching to a single-payer system like Canada's would be 9 percent, or, in current expenditures, about a billion dollars. The GAO concluded, "If the . . . single-payer features of the Canadian system were applied in the United States, the savings in administrative costs alone would be more than enough to finance insurance coverage for the millions of Americans who are currently uninsured. There would be enough left over to permit a reduction, or possibly even the elimination, of co-payments and deductibles [for the insured and uninsured], if that were deemed appropriate." The GAO conclusions would be just as valid for an American-style single-payer run by Medicare.

Other studies have reported that the administrative savings (for insurer and provider overhead combined) achievable by an American single-payer system may be higher than the 9 percent derived by the GAO, possibly as high as 15 percent.

Therefore, Americans should ignore pleas from "ethicists" to debate health care rationing until such time as we have debated whether we want our health care dollars being used to pay for Blue Cross Blue Shield advertisements and HMO doctor police rather than, say, bone marrow transplants for poor kids with leukemia or hip replacement operations for elderly people with fractured hips.

Allowing Hospitals to Make End-of-Life Decisions Leads to the Mistreatment of Vulnerable Patients

by Wesley J. Smith

About the author: *Wesley J. Smith is an attorney and consultant for the International Task Force on Euthanasia and Assisted Suicide. He is also the author of numerous books and articles on medical ethics.*

[Since the 1990s,] "futilitarians" have been busily redefining the role of doctors, the ethics of health care, the perceived moral worth of sick and disabled people, and the power of patients over their own bodies. Their theory goes something like this: when a patient reaches a certain stage of age, illness, or injury, any further treatment other than comfort care is "futile" and should be withheld or withdrawn. That the patient may want the treatment because of deeply held values or a desire to live longer or take a chance on medical improvement is not decisive; the doctors and hospitals involved have the right to refuse treatment as an exercise of *their* autonomy.

All of this begs the question: which treatments are futile? That is a matter that bioethicists and other members of the medical intelligentsia are still debating, but like a picture downloading from the Internet via a low capacity modem, a rough bioethical consensus is coming slowly into focus.

Defining Futility

In May 1994, Dr. Marcia Angell, executive editor of the *New England Journal of Medicine*, wrote that patients diagnosed as permanently unconscious should be refused medical treatment so that "demoralized" caregivers would not be forced to provide care they believe is futile or wastes "valuable resources." How? One way suggested by Dr. Angell would be to change the definition of "death" to include a diagnosis of permanent unconsciousness. Realizing the public relations issues inherent in declaring a breathing body a corpse, Dr. Angell declared that she would also accept the creation of mandatory time limits on providing medical treatment for unconscious people, after which the care would be withdrawn regardless of family objections. Her third and preferred approach would be to negate the usual legal presumption in favor of life, thereby forcing families with the "idiosyncratic view" that their loved one should be provided treatment to prove in court that the patient would want such care.

By the time Angell's editorial was published, Daniel Callahan, one of the godfathers of bioethics, had already offered several rather vague definitions of medical futility in his 1993 book, *The Troubled Dream of Life*. It exists, he wrote, when:

• "there is a likely, though not necessarily certain, downward course of an illness, making death a strong probability"; or,

• "successful treatment is more likely to bring extended unconsciousness or advanced dementia than cure or significant amelioration"; or,

• "the available treatments for a potentially fatal condition entail a significant likelihood of extended pain or suffering"; or,

• "the available treatments significantly increase the probability of a bad death, even if they promise to extend life."

In such cases, Callahan urged that a presumption be created against medical treatment other than comfort care, and that people who insist on this "futile" treatment be required to pay for it themselves.

The American Thoracic Society (chest doctors) embraced Futile Care Theory early on, issuing a policy statement declaring that treatment should be considered futile "if reasoning and experience indicate that the intervention would be highly unlikely to result in a *meaningful* survival for the patient" (their emphasis), and also asserting that a "health care institution has the right to limit a life-sustaining intervention without consent."

Why Futile Care Is Dangerous

While the ultimate definition of futile care has not yet been agreed upon within bioethics and the medical community, many hospitals and doctors are already putting theory into practice. That being so, the time has come to expose the dangers of this emerging medical philosophy.

Futility is a value judgment, not a medical determination. Medical futility used to be an objective medical determination that a proposed treatment could have virtually no physiological benefit to the patient. To illustrate the point with an extreme example: if a patient asks a doctor for an appendectomy to cure an ear infection, the physician is—and should be—obligated by professional ethics to refuse the request. This "objective" concept of futility is not, however, what Futile Care Theory is all about. Rather, when futilitarians use the terms "medical futility," "inappropriate care," or "nonbeneficial treatment," they have entered the realm of subjective value judgments. As Dr. Stuart Youngner, a bioethicist and medical professor at Case Western Reserve University School of Medicine, put it, "futility determinations will inevitably involve value judgments about: 1) whether low probability chances are worth taking; and 2) whether certain lives are of a quality worth living."

Determinations about futility involve paternalism. "Medical paternalism exists," writes the medical ethicist Edmund D. Pellegrino, MD, "when the physician assumes the patient's right to make self-governing decisions and acts to prevent, manipulate, or coerce him or her in the name of the patient's best interests." That was exactly what was wrong with hooking people up to medical machines against their will. Now, with futility, a new and more deadly game of "Doctor Knows Best" is being played, and this time, instead of compelling lives to be extended, the doctor decides that the time has come for the patient to die—whether or not the patient agrees.

The Example of Ethyl

The inherent arrogance of strangers imposing futility determinations upon family members and patients was well illustrated in a revealing story in *California Lawyer* written by a former house counsel to Stanford University Hospital, about a woman named Ethyl who had been receiving kidney dialysis there for several years and had entered end-stage renal disease. Ethyl was very ill: a diabetic with cardiac problems, she was bloated from fluid buildup caused by her kidney failure.

Ethyl was cared for by her daughter, Mary. Hospital workers noticed that during her treatments, Ethyl seemed "agitated and distressed" but she never "was able to voice any specific complaints or requests." After one dialysis session left her weak and "unable to move from the dialysis couch to the wheelchair," her urologist decided that the treatment was too difficult for her. He tried to convince Mary to discontinue the dialysis and limit treatment to comfort care.

> *"Futility decisions will be based on prejudice and bias against disabled people or other minorities."*

When Mary refused, doctors and hospital staffers launched an intense pressure campaign to convince her to cease her mother's life-sustaining treatment. As the months passed, members of the medical team groused that Mary had become "hostile to everyone in the center and threatened legal action if they did not continue her mother's treatments." Is it any wonder? The staff's refusal to take no for an answer transformed the patient/physician partnership into an adversary relationship.

Unable to impose his will on Mary, Ethyl's doctor took the issue to the hospi-

46

tal biomedical ethics committee, chaired by a "medical ethicist" with "philosophical and medical training" and consisting of nurses, physicians, caseworkers, and community representatives. The committee picked apart Mary's supposed motives for wanting her mother to live. It determined that Mary "was a loving and attentive caregiver" but found "no evidence" that Ethyl "had ever expressed her own preferences about medical treatment." Mary had religious beliefs, which may have been affecting her decision making. "Committee members with training in social services and psychology" asked about Mary's relationship with her mother and were told that she had "few friends" and that Ethyl's death would leave Mary "alone and without a focus."

The ethics committee decided that "Mary's own needs were interfering with her ability to act in her mother's best interest," and further determined "that the burdens of Ethyl's treatment more than likely outweighed the benefits." The ethics committee told the doctor to try to transfer care to another physician, and if that failed, to stop treatment unilaterally.

A few weeks later, the committee convened to discuss Ethyl's case. To everyone's surprise, Mary had found a doctor willing to continue her mother's dialysis. Thwarted in their desire to impose their values on Ethyl's situation, one member said bitterly, "The poor woman, her daughter is blind to what is best for her."

Some might call this a happy ending, for it permitted a loving daughter to determine her mother's care rather than strangers steeped in amoral bioethics training. Yet frighteningly, the "loophole" Mary used to ensure her mother's continued treatment—getting another doctor to treat in the same facility—has been closed by some hospital futile care policy protocols, which refuse a new doctor permission to render treatment that the hospital ethics committee has proclaimed to be futile.

Changing the Doctor-Patient Relationship

Futility decisions will be based on prejudice and bias against disabled people or other minorities. This may already be happening. The Mayo Clinic has reported that many physicians' definition of futility "includes interventions that might be considered medically reasonable." The report noted that some of the doctors studied wanted to refuse CPR even if the patient's chance of survival "was 10 percent or greater." Moreover, the potential for futility decisions being based on the physician's prejudice or bias is clearly illustrated by the findings of one medical study that *"CPR was more likely to be considered futile if the patient was not white"* (my emphasis).

Futile Care Theory gives some of medicine's most important health care decisions to strangers. Deciding whether to accept or reject life-sustaining care is one of the most difficult medical choices patients and families will ever have to make. Indeed, when bioethicists argue that families should be able to discontinue tube feeding for cognitively disabled family members, they commonly speak of protecting family intimacy and personal values. But when faced with decisions they disagree with, considerations of intimacy and patient values take second place to institutional and professional values.

The trend transforming hospital biomedical ethics committees from mediators of controversies between doctors and patients into life-and-death decision makers is only one example of this growing medical depersonalization. The emergence of a new medical specialist known as the "hospitalist" is another. Hospitalists are physicians assigned to direct the overall medical care of hospitalized patients: they interact with treating specialists, decide when to admit and discharge patients, and assume the other medical duties that traditionally have been the responsibility of the patient's personal physician. This means that a patient sick enough to be hospitalized will not be under the care of the doctor they may have known for years, even though it is at just such a time that the link of trust forged over many years between patient and doctor is most important.

"Futile Care Theory illustrates the incremental approach with which bioethics corrodes traditional medical ethics."

Hospitalists are not paid by patients; they are employees of the hospital in which they work, or independent consultants who have contracted to provide hospitalist services. A major purpose of the hospitalist movement is to reduce costs and improve efficiency without compromising quality of care. These are certainly worthy goals. But hospitalists will also become major providers of end-of-life care. That could help improve pain and symptom control, since many family doctors and internists have inadequate training in end-of-life care. But the emergence of hospitalists is very worrisome in the context of Futile Care Theory. They will be virtual strangers to the patient and family, and their primary emotional loyalty, albeit not necessarily their professional responsibility, is likely to be to their institution. This could leave marginalized patients at material risk of being written off as futile care cases. This worry is heightened when advocates of the hospitalist movement urge practitioners to obtain "superb training in biomedical ethics."

HMOs [health maintenance organizations] already induce physicians to keep costs low, using a combination of financial rewards or punishments, which create at least an implicit conflict of interest between doctors and some patients. Futile Care Theory takes this disturbing trend a step further. Indeed, some futile care supporters argue that the Hippocratic tradition of individual loyalty must give way to a new medical ethic in which physician loyalty is divided between the individual patient and the entire patient group for which they are responsible. In such a milieu, some will receive optimal care, others will not; some will have access to the treatment they desire, others will be cut off unilaterally. Futile care proponents go so far as to argue that if the "community" decides that specified care should be withheld, such a decision trumps the needs and desires of the individual. Such policies would break the back of Hippocratic medicine, endangering the lives of the most vulnerable (and expensive) patients.

Making the Unthinkable Inevitable

Futile Care Theory illustrates the incremental approach with which bioethics corrodes traditional medical ethics. When Dr. Leo Alexander warned of the dangers of utilitarianism in medicine fifty years ago, he had no idea that the bioethics movement would intentionally push the profession away from the values of Hippocratic medicine. Nor did he know that the changes he feared would be instituted by deliberate design, as incremental "reform." But that is what has happened. A once "unthinkable" practice is rendered debatable by being respectfully discussed in bioethics and medical journals. Soon, a few cases occur in which the new approach is applied. Eventually, what was formerly controversial becomes a regular part of clinical practice, creating a new ethical paradigm. Finally, the once unthinkable act or omission may actually become the required decision.

That is certainly the pattern in cases of diagnosed persistent unconsciousness. First, dehydration, once unthinkable, was promoted as a matter of respecting patient and family treatment choices, i.e., the right to die. Dehydration was applied against a few patients at the request of family, to general approval in the courts, culminating in the Cruzan case.[1] Soon, dehydration of people in PVS [persistent vegetative state] became a relatively ho-hum clinical practice. Now, with Futile Care Theory, some hospital protocols *require* feeding tubes to be withdrawn from PVS patients, even *over the objections* of family decision makers and in spite of patient desires expressed in advance medical directives. Indeed, Dr. Ronald Cranford, the neurologist/bioethicist who promoted dehydration in the Cruzan,

> *"Hospital biomedical ethics committees . . . have few checks or balances placed upon them."*

Michael Martin, and Robert Wendland cases, has acknowledged that these changes "proceeded" in this "logical and incremental way." Further, Cranford expects the same pattern to unfold in the futility debate, although he expects the wrangling to be "more complex and controversial" than was the argument over whether it should be ethical to withhold food and fluids.

Some doctors and hospitals already refuse wanted care based on Futile Care Theory. These decisions are based on two slightly differing approaches. Let's call them "process futility" and "defined futility." Process futility uses bureaucratic procedure to empower doctors to refuse care. As described in the August

---

1. Nancy Cruzan was a Missouri woman who got into a car accident that left her without any significant cognitive function. Her family sought to have her artificial feeding and hydration equipment withdrawn but was refused by the Missouri Supreme Court. The U.S. Supreme Court affirmed the lower court's ruling.

21, 1996 *Journal of the American Medical Association* (JAMA), some Houston hospitals have already implemented process futility protocols created by a collaboration of area hospital ethics committees. (According to the JAMA report, the protocols permit "professional integrity and institutional integrity" to counterbalance "patient autonomy.") The Houston policy created an eight-step "conflict resolution mechanism"—essentially a quasi-adversary system between doctors and patients—in which ethics committees are granted the ultimate power to decide disputes when doctors want to refuse continued treatment (other than comfort care) as "inappropriate" and patients or families refuse to go along. Under the protocol, once the ethics committee issues its decision, the matter is settled and all further "inappropriate" care may be terminated unilaterally.

Defined futility protocols get to the same place—denying wanted treatment—through a somewhat different route: stipulating in advance the specific medical conditions for which treatment is deemed futile. This approach seeks to bring consistency into futile care decision making, and improve the chances that patients and families will acquiesce to futility determinations since they are based on preestablished rules, while offering bereaved families the cold comfort of knowing that the refusal of wanted care was not a personal rejection.

The Bureaucracy of Futile Care

The Alexian Brothers Hospital of San Jose, California, promulgated such a defined futility policy (Non-beneficial Treatment) in February 1997. Its stated purpose: "to promote a positive atmosphere of comfort care for patients near the end of life" and to ensure that the dying process not be "unnecessarily prolonged"—a matter the hospital determines, not patients or families.

The Alexian Brothers policy presumes that requests for medical treatment or testing, including CPR, are "inappropriate" for a person with any of the following conditions:
• Irreversible coma, persistent vegetative state, or anencephaly.
• Permanent dependence on intensive care to sustain life.
• Terminal illness with neurological, renal, oncological, or other devastating disease.
• Untreatable lethal congenital abnormality.
• Severe, irreversible dementia.
The only treatment these patients are entitled to receive is comfort care.

Even though the Alexian Brothers policy defines the conditions for which continued medical treatment is deemed inappropriate, bureaucratic processes remain important. If the patient or family "insists on continuing 'inappropriate' treatment after being advised that it is nonbeneficial," the case is sent to the biomedical ethics committee. "If the recommendations of the bioethics committee are not accepted by the patient (or surrogate) care should be transferred to another institution." And if, as is often the case, no other institution is willing to take the patient? Again the policy is silent, but one suspects, as in the Houston futility policy, that care will be refused despite patient and family desires.

Both the Houston and the San Jose Alexian Brothers futile care policies illustrate the growing power that is being given to biomedical ethics committees, including in some cases the power to make life-and-death treatment decisions. This is a profoundly dangerous development. Hospital biomedical ethics committees were originally established to craft hospital ethics protocols, give informal advice in difficult ethical situations, and mediate disputes between patients, families, and professional caregivers, they were not created to be quasi-judicial determiners of treatment disputes. Thus they have few checks or balances placed upon them—a necessary precaution with any meaningful exercise of power. Membership in the committees is anonymous, and no uniform criteria exist to qualify. Deliberations are confidential, and written records detailing committee reasoning often are not maintained. Ethics committee decisions are usually not included in medical charts. There are no performance reviews or formalized methods for objective oversight. There is no formal appeals process. Individual members generally cannot be questioned later in court about their assessments, conclusions, or the deliberative process itself. The potential for abuse due to prejudice, inadequate information, ideological zeal, or incompetence is so pronounced that ethics committees could become the medical equivalent of Star Chambers.[2]

---

2. The Star Chamber was a sixteenth- and seventeenth-century British court known for its unfair proceedings.

Health Maintenance Organizations Must Learn to Act Ethically

by James L. Connor

About the author: *James L. Connor is the director of the Woodstock Theological Center at Georgetown University.*

All of a sudden, the managed health care system in the United States finds itself at roughly the same berth of popularity as tobacco companies, gun manufacturers, and asbestos makers. Managed care executives are getting cast as the bad guys in television dramas and movies like "As Good As It Gets," which has become an icon of the near-universal loathing of these Health Maintenance Organizations.

There are surely some venal people in managed care, as there are in all sectors of society, including organized religion. What the HMO horror shows usually overlook, however, is that these executives are operating in one of the more excruciating moral mazes of contemporary American business. As a priest and ethicist who reaches out to business leaders, I have come to know a fair number of them. As a whole, they're very decent people who want to do the right thing. But they work in a corporate culture that often transcends, and trumps, their deepest values.

Not Like Other Businesses

The bane of healthcare today is the illusion that it's a business like any other. According to this fallacy, delivering healthcare is like making widgets or Nike sneakers. Most people, of course, don't think so. That's because the encounter between patient and provider is not simply an economic transaction. It's a human interaction, a relationship of care. It strikes at the very essence of human well-being. My friends in managed care understand this, on some deep level.

But they also understand the game they're in, and must play by its rules. In business, that means competition and the drive toward market share and profits or revenue (pressures applying to nonprofit as well as for-profit systems in today's healthcare environment).

The paradox is that by playing this game so exceedingly well, HMOs are losing it. Congress is wielding a bipartisan hammer of legislation, physicians are unionizing, and the specter of costly malpractice lawsuits is haunting managed care organizations.

What managed care could use is a careful dose of moral perspective, for its own survival as well as for the greater good. My general prescription is a strong institutional sense that the business of healthcare is not business; it's care of health. Decision-makers in the system need to begin cultivating the habit of ethical deliberation; and for that, they need a corporate climate that encourages discussion of their dilemmas. HMO horror stories aside, these are indeed moral dilemmas. The cases that come before these people are usually resistant to easy moralizing.

How does one deliberate over decisions that can so rapidly descend into HMO hell? One key is to focus on the "how" of decision-making, not just the "what" or results. The public has tended to dwell on yes-or-no decisions in contested cases of managed care, involving medical procedures such as Autologous Bone Marrow Transplants for women with advanced breast cancer and Lung Volume Reduction Surgery for patients with advanced chronic pulmonary disease. But all of us, especially healthcare providers, should give greater ethical import to the value-laden process of arriving at those decisions.

A Fictional Illustration

Let's examine a composite case:

Eight-year-old Jason Martin has a deadly brain tumor and one last hope: a new cancer-fighting drug being tested several hundred miles away. The Martins, a family of modest means, have health insurance through a managed care organization. But the regional treatment center is outside the network of providers, and the organization has refused to cover the costly, experimental drug therapy. With Jason's story hitting the press, an appeal by the parents has landed on the desk of Dr. Stanley, a medical director with a solid commitment to delivering high-quality, appropriate care. What should he do?

The account—though fictional—is of the kind that has turned public wrath on the HMO industry. At the Woodstock Theological Center at Georgetown University in Washington, we brought together 54 healthcare practitioners, industry leaders, and policy experts, who grappled with scenarios like this one. They met periodically for seminar-style meetings [between 1998 and 2000], checking the ethical pulse of managed care.

The moral drama of Jason Martin's case lies in the medical director's methodical mulling of questions that spotlight often-colliding values and priorities. For example, Dr. Stanley's managed care organization has a policy of not covering treatment that is experimental or outside the network of providers. Would granting an exception in Jason's case create a harmful precedent? Would more patients insist on exotic and unproven procedures, possibly escalating the costs of employee health plans? Would employers pass on the charges to their workers, or trim health benefits to hold down costs? The organization's oncologists have begun testing the same cancer-fighting drug, though less promisingly than at the regional center. Would a choice to send the family outside the network betray a lack of confidence in Dr. Stanley's own staff?

Furthermore, have Jason's parents really weighed the slender chance of success, against the burden of further treatment and the hardship of separation during what might be their son's final days? The regional center is 400 miles away, and Jason's father would have to stay behind at his job.

> *"What managed care could use is a careful dose of moral perspective."*

During seminar meetings, participants acted the parts of these and other "stakeholders." In the end, Dr. Stanley decides to cover the experimental treatment—but only within the network. He also decides to tap the regional center's physician as a consultant. (The panelist who role-played the good doctor is, in fact, a medical director of a large managed care organization.) "It came down to a gut feeling, based on limited evidence he had, that Jason might have a chance to get an additional 24 months of life with the new therapy," the panel said in its report titled "Ethical Issues in Managed Health Care Organizations" (published by Georgetown University Press).

Did Dr. Stanley make the right choice? I don't know; I suspect there wasn't a single "right choice" in this case. What I find more revealing is the process of ethical decision-making that yielded this result. Essentially, what the medical director did was probe the legitimate claims—and values—of the various so-called stakeholders. These include patients and their families, physicians, employers who sponsor health plans, and, in the case of for-profit systems, shareholders. Such a process needs to become the norm, not the exception, in managed care. That is, if it wants to rekindle the trust of all stakeholders and the larger public.

Creating an Ethical Framework

Obviously, HMOs won't foster this habit of ethical deliberation as long as they cling to the illusion that healthcare is just a business, trading in a precious commodity. All healthcare leaders and practitioners must think of themselves as pursuing not just a career but a calling—a "profession" in the venerable sense of the word. Institutionally, managed care organizations can drive home the message, and steer the case-by-case deliberations, with functional mission statements. These statements must say plainly that the goal of healthcare is caring for health. Everything else, including shareholder return and executive compensation, should be understood as practical means toward the delivery of quality healthcare rather than as ends unto themselves.

Within such an explicitly ethical framework, managed care must also build a corporate culture of transparency. This could conceivably take the public form of annual "ethical audits" ranking the values and priorities that drive decision-making and, within limits of confidentiality, disclosing how tough cases got resolved. Openness and transparency can be the salvation of managed care at a time when the system seems hell-bound in the public's judgment.

Amid the groundswell of demand for a "Patients' Bill of Rights," we should also remember that patients have responsibilities, too. They have an obligation to understand that medical resources are finite, and that exotic treatment often has diminishing returns, especially in the final months of life. Ultimately, patients need to factor death into the human equation. Organized religion has a distinct role in preaching this word to cantankerous patients who can't accept death, because they really haven't accepted life. Death does not have the last word in the unbounded book of life.

Though there may be fictional strands in the recent stories of HMO horror, these tales reveal an institution in crisis. It is a crisis of moral legitimacy. The ethical fortunes of this ailing system may well depend on how many real-life Dr. Stanleys are out there in the brave new world of managed care.

Chapter 2

What Ethics Should Guide Organ Transplants?

Chapter Preface

In October 2000 National Basketball Association star Alonzo Mourning announced that he had a kidney disease. He continued to play for several more seasons, retiring temporarily in November 2003 due to poor kidney function. On December 19, 2003, Mourning received a kidney from a second cousin. The public's response to Mourning's health problems helps to shed light on the ethics of organ transplants, especially when the patient is a celebrity.

Mourning's announcement affected his fans deeply, to the extent that dozens of them offered to donate their kidneys to the basketball star. Although Mourning eventually received a kidney from a family member, his plight still generated questions about the whole process of organ donations. Because the vast majority of people in need of transplants do not receive as many offers as the famous athlete did, some people wonder whether celebrities have an unfair advantage when it comes to receiving a new organ. However, the guidelines designed by hospitals and the procedures set up by the United Network for Organ Sharing help to ensure that organs from nonfamily donors are distributed fairly, based on the location of the organ donors and the relative health of the patients—not on how well known the patient is. In addition, as philosophy professor Ronald Munson argues in his book about organ transplants, *Raising the Dead*, "Celebrities in our society are awarded special privileges so often that one need not be cynical to suspect every benefit they receive is unmerited. But it's easy to forget celebrities can also fall sick with life-threatening diseases. When that happens, they're entitled to be treated the same as everyone else."

More importantly, Mourning's stardom proved to be a boon to organ donations as a whole. Beyond offering to donate their kidneys, his fans and others who had heard of Mourning's plight began to inquire about the general need for organ donations and ways they could help others in Mourning's situation. Several columnists praised the generosity of these potential donors. *Sports Illustrated* columnist Rick Reilly profiled several of the people who had initially offered their kidneys to Mourning and who later decided they would give them to others with similar afflictions. Reilly notes, "In truth, Mourning's fame won't just save his life, it'll save hundreds of lives."

Alonzo Mourning's NBA career has not ended, despite the transplant. He made a comeback in the 2004–05 season, though it is unclear how much longer his career will continue. The debate surrounding Mourning's fame and his organ transplant surgery is an example of the ethical issues that surround organ donations. Those issues, including whether organs should be sold and whether animals can help alleviate the organ shortage, are evaluated by the authors in the following chapter.

Animal-to-Human Transplants Will Save Lives

by Ronald Munson

About the author: *Ronald Munson is a professor of philosophy at the University of Missouri–St. Louis.*

In W.W. Jacob's classic horror story *The Monkey's Paw*, elderly couple coming into possession of a mummified monkey hand with magical properties realize with a thrill of excitement that by using its power they can resurrect their recently dead son.

But when the mangled corpse of their boy lurches up the walk and starts pounding on the front door; the father sees they have made a terrible mistake.

The Potential Dangers of Xenotransplantation

An obvious lesson of the story is that we should be cautious about translating our dreams into reality. The unintended consequences of getting what we wish for may face us with the prospect of desperately attempting to reverse a horrible result.

Many critics are opposed to seeing the dream of xenotransplantation realized. Some reject it for exploiting animals, while others spurn it for blurring the line between humans and beasts. Both criticisms express legitimate ethical concerns (although I find neither persuasive), but they and similar worries pale in significance when compared to the question of the public-health hazard posed by xenotransplantation.

An unusual aspect of xenotransplantation as a therapy is that the risk associated with it isn't limited to the patient. In the middle decades of the twentieth century, when surgeons were experimenting with transplanting human donor organs, only the recipients were taking a chance. If someone believed getting a donor liver might save her life, she could decide to take the gamble. When the liver failed, the outcome was sad, but only the recipient died.

Xenotransplantation can potentially affect an indefinite number of other people. If a recipient becomes infected with a lethal virus, the infection could spread, striking others not directly involved. Transplanting animal organs into people may thus put us all at risk. It would be irresponsible for us to follow the pattern of the past and leave decisions about xenografts to surgeons and their patients.

Everyone has a stake in the outcome.

The fundamental ethical question about xenotransplantation, in my view, is whether we should proceed with it. Imagining the problem of hyperacute rejection [when the human body rejects the animal organ] brought under control, do we want to risk the public-health consequences of putting animal organs into people? Should we even go forward with clinical trials? . . .

No Signs of Disease

We can try looking to the past as a guide to determining future risks. We're not completely without experience. Perhaps three hundred or so transplants of animal organs have been performed since the start of the twentieth century, most using primate donors. So have these animal organs produced an infectious disease in any of the recipients?

Apparently not.

This seems reassuring, because transplants of human donor organs are known to produce infections. Hepatitis B, C, and G, herpes viruses, a single-stranded DNA virus called TTV, and HIV are among those that have slipped through the screening process and been transmitted to patients.

The most recent virus known to be passed on by infected organs is HHV-8, which causes Kaposi's sarcoma, a cancer of the skin and organ linings. For those infected with HIV, because of weakened immune systems, Kaposi's sarcoma is often the first visible sign of AIDS.

Yet the lack of disease in xenograft recipients may be false reassurance. The recipients have usually died quickly, the animal organs remaining in their bodies only a few hours or days in most cases, a few weeks or months in a handful of others. Such times may be too short for mutations or recombinations to occur. Past cases thus can't tell us much about what might happen if an animal organ stays in contact with human cells for several years.

But another part of the past that might guide us is the human contact with pig viruses.

Studies of Pig Viruses

Humans have been exposed to pig viruses in numerous cell-to-cell contacts. Pig skin has been used for decades to cover serious burns, pig pancreatic islet cells are implanted to treat diabetes, and pig livers periodically serve as bridges for patients waiting for donor livers. Pig kidneys have been employed for external dialysis and spleens used in attempts at immunotherapy. Several hundred people have also been given implants of pig neural tissue to treat them for neurological damage or diseases, including Parkinson's.

Scientists are only now studying the consequences of such pig-to-human exposure. German researchers, in the most worrisome cases, discovered that PERV [porcine endogenal retrovirus] particles can be released from pig endothelial cells. What's more, when the pig cells are cultured with human embryonic kidney cells, the human cells become infected with PERV.

> *"People are dying every day whose lives might be saved by xenotransplants."*

But other results tell a different story. In a study of ten patients given islet cells between 1990 and 1993, Swedish scientists found swine influenza virus in all ten. Although five tested positive for pig parvoviruses and five for other pig viruses, only one person had become ill and tests for PERV were negative.

In a study in St. Petersburg, Russia, 23 of 100 patients whose blood had been perfused through a pig spleen for one hour as long as eight years previously still had pig cells in their blood, although none tested positive for PERV. Researchers from Imutran, in another study, examined 160 patients treated with pig tissue implants at hospitals throughout the world and discovered no infections caused by pig viruses.

The studies so far are generally reassuring. But there's a limit to their usefulness. HIV may have crossed into humans only once, and no study of pig viruses in people can demonstrate that such an event will never happen again. It may even have happened already without our knowing about it yet.

Deadly Proteins

Viruses aren't the only worry, and here too the past may serve as a guide. In 1956 injections of human growth hormone became a standard therapy for children failing to develop properly. The hormone was extracted from the pituitary glands of people recently dead.

Not until thirty years later, when a few patients developed the symptoms of the brain disorder Creutzfeldt-Jakob disease (CJD), did researchers realize that the extracts used to treat them must have been contaminated with an infectious agent with a long incubation period

The agent causing CJD is a protein structure called a prion. It's the same sort of agent that causes mad-cow disease (bovine spongiform encephalopathy, or BSE), the brain disease which has particularly affected the cattle herds in European counties, Britain in particular, and been responsible for the death of more than a hundred people.

No one could have screened for prions in 1956, because their existence wasn't suspected. Also, the long lapse between infection and the occurrence of symptoms made it impossible to stop or modify a therapy that was infecting more and more people. We know now that Creutzfeldt-Jakob disease is also associated with the transplantation of corneas and dura mater (the tough tissue covering the brain) from infected donors. Only if the signs of CJD have appeared in a potential donor, however, is it possible to avoid transmitting the disease to a recipient.

Pressure to Conduct Clinical Trials

Pressures are building, even in the midst of debates about safety, to initiate clinical trials of xenotransplants. Why the hurry? One persuasive answer is that people are dying every day whose lives might be saved by xenotransplants.

While this is true, critics see the rush toward clinical trials as driven by pressures exerted by multinational corporations. Imutran (a subsidiary of the Swiss company Novartis Pharm AG) and Nextran (owned by Baxter International, a medical-products manufacturer) are among those that have invested large sums in trying to develop xenotransplantation into a reliable therapy.

The shortage of human donors, an aging population, and the needs of cultures like Japan's that discourage organ donation add up to a huge potential market for transplantable pig organs. The market, by some estimates, is worth six billion dollars and can be expected to grow. With so much money in prospect, critics charge, corporations may be tempted to minimize public-health risks and push ahead with clinical trials.

Nor are the corporations alone in this. Patient advocacy groups and some transplant surgeons are also eager to initiate clinical trials. Pressure may be greatest from people pressing for cell transplants. Parkinson's, Huntington's, and Alzheimer's diseases, multiple sclerosis, diabetes, stroke, and brain injury are among the disorders that could benefit from implants of the right sort of animal cells.

Clinical trials of cell transplants have been underway in the United States (with FDA approval) since 1996, and some results have been encouraging. Parkinson's patients, in particular, have shown marked improvement when treated with injections of pig neural cells. Treatments for diabetes haven't been successful, though, and the results from the Huntington's trials are still being assessed. The other treatment possibilities remain at the stage of animal studies.

Transplanted cells lack the GAL-sugar [galactose-alpha,1,3-galactose] found in the lining of blood vessels. Thus cells, unlike organs, don't have to cope with hyperacute rejection and are more likely to be tolerated. Yet, although cell implants may benefit patients, the public health risk from animal cells (whatever it is) seems the same as that posed by organs.

Two Arguments Against Xenotransplantation

The basic ethical question about xenotransplantation, I said earlier, is whether to proceed with it. Are we, as a society, willing to take unknown risks to offer the potential benefits of xenografts and cell implants to those who have a serious, perhaps even life-threatening, need?

Some researchers and ethicists say no. Worried about unintended and unforseen consequences, they favor what I call the monkey's-paw position. That is, they consider going forward with xenografts as too dangerous and advocate a moratorium. Two strong arguments support their position.

The Trigger Argument

Premise 1 The risk of triggering an epidemic of an AIDS-like disease is unknown but real.

Premise 2 Transplanting animal materials (organs or cells) into humans, even if successful, would help relatively few people.

Conclusion We are risking the lives of millions of people to help (at best) only a comparative few.

Given that the prime justification for using xenografts is to save lives, the trigger argument suggests that continuing to test xenografts would frustrate this end. It would be like trying to put out a fire with kerosene. While it might be possible, we risk losing a great many more lives than we save. The argument thus supports the further conclusion that we should declare a moratorium on xenografts until we can assess the risk we're taking to help the people who might benefit.

Consent Argument

The consent argument, like the trigger argument, invokes our ignorance of the risk xenografts pose.

Premise 1 The risk of triggering an epidemic of an AIDS-like disease is unknown but real.

Premise 2 Clinical trials of xenografts subject the entire population, not just the patients, to risk.

Conclusion We who are not patients are thus being put at risk without our consent.

Like the trigger argument, the consent argument supports the additional conclusion that we ought to declare a moratorium on xenografts. This would permit us not only to assess the risk, but to decide whether we want to take it. The power of the argument comes from the idea that clinical trials of xenografts turn us all into research subjects, even though we've never been informed of our risks or consented to participate.

A Moratorium Is Not the Answer

I'm one of many who reject the monkey's-paw view in favor of what I'll call the rickety-bridge position. Because xenografts can save lives, they take us where we want to go, and it would be a mistake to declare a moratorium on them. Yet they are admittedly a rickety and potentially dangerous bridge, and we need to gather data to assess their danger, even as we continue to creep forward.

The factors favoring a moratorium are powerful, but I think three considerations ultimately outweigh them. Before discussing them, I'll state them as the premises of an argument.

Lives-Saved Argument

Premise 1 A moratorium on xenografts would result in the death of people who otherwise might be saved.

Premise 2 Patients with diabetes or neurological disorders like Parkinson's disease would be denied the potential benefit of animal-cell implants.

Premise 3 We would reduce only marginally the chance of an epidemic of a novel, AIDS-like infectious disease.

Conclusion By imposing a moratorium, we would be buying only relative safety and paying too high a price in lives and (potential) benefits for it.

Lives Lost and Suffering Continued

Premise 1 While triggering of an epidemic by a xenograft is a realistic possibility, no one believes it's more than slightly probable. In considering whether to adopt a moratorium, we thus must balance the slender likelihood of a catastrophic plague against the virtual certainty of the death of hundreds (perhaps eventually thousands) of people. I recommend we favor real people who will surely die over those we imagine dying in the remote event of an epidemic.

Those certain to die who otherwise might be saved are people needing the temporary support provided by an animal liver. (Animal hearts have never been used successfully this way, and dialysis has made relying on animal kidneys unnecessary, but the use of an animal liver can sometimes make the difference between life and death.) If surgeons are forbidden by a moratorium to use a pig liver to bridge the gap between the time a patient's liver fails and the time a human donor liver is located, many patients will die. Nor can they be saved by the use of artificial-liver machines, because such machines employ pig liver cells to do their job.

"So far as we can tell, no adverse effects have resulted [from xenografts]."

An obvious implication of Premise 1 is that attempting to secure complete safety from an epidemic by imposing a moratorium has to be paid for in human lives.

Premise 2 Premise 2 indicates that death isn't the only human price a moratorium would exact. People with neurological disorders, diabetes, and spinal-cord injuries would be denied any potential benefit of animal-cell transplant therapy. The therapy is now more of a promise than an established treatment, but for some people it offers the only realistic hope of bettering their lives. What's more, a moratorium would be a barrier to further efforts to improve cell-implant therapy, which holds more immediate promise than animal organ transplants.

Premise 3 That viruses repeatedly and unpredictably cross from other species into ours suggests that a moratorium on xenografts would have little value in reducing the chance of an HIV-like epidemic. Viruses cross from one species to another, and we can do little or nothing to prevent it. Species jumping happens often with flu viruses, yet it's a rare occurrence for an alien invader to produce a disease like the English Sweating Sickness or the Spanish Influenza. It's even rarer, fortunately, for an invading virus to cause a disease like AIDS.

Whether we like it or not, our species is inescapably involved in nature's genetic experiments, and it's an illusion to think that by forbidding xenografts we can gain safety from epidemics of novel diseases. The best we can accomplish is to reduce marginally the present likelihood of one occurring, but to achieve even this anemic result, we'd have to pay for it in lost lives and delayed (or abandoned) treatments for diseases needing better therapies.

Reasonable people may differ about whether the cost of a moratorium is worth the protection it provides, but in making that reckoning, everyone needs to consider that a moratorium exacts a price. It's one measured in human lives and suffering and in promising therapies postponed.

Preserving Lives and Minimizing Dangers

How can a defender of the rickety-bridge view respond to the argument that clinical trials of xenografts put us at risk without our consent? I think we can admit it's true, but not have to agree a moratorium is justified.

No one knows exactly how much risk xenografts expose us to, but we've been exposed to it for a least a century. So far as we can tell, no adverse effects have resulted. It's true one could occur at any moment, but that's been so since the time Emrich Ullmann attached the pig kidney to his patient's blood vessels. Xenografts are merely one of the more-or-less constant background risks we face all the time.

This isn't to say we shouldn't take steps to minimize whatever risk xenografts involve. That this should be done is part of the rickety-bridge position. The idea is to preserve and improve lives, while protecting against risk in every reasonable way possible.

Animal-to-Human Transplantation Is Dangerous and Immoral

by Dan Lyons

About the author: *Dan Lyons is the director of Uncaged Campaigns, an antivivisection organization based in Great Britain.*

The last hundred years has witnessed many attempts to carry out animal-to-human organ transplants—all have failed. Pigs are now being genetically manipulated to carry human genes in the hope that this catalogue of failure and misery can be turned into a viable medical treatment. Approximately 6,000 people are on the waiting lists for human organs: does xenotransplantation offer them real hope, or might it be one of the greatest medical disasters of all time?

The Health Risks of Xenotransplantation

We do not yet know the functions of all human genes and we have identified only a tiny fraction of pigs' DNA, yet xenotransplantation scientists are combining the two and planning to introduce the results directly into the human body. We are, literally, interfering with something we do not understand. What we do know is that pigs and humans both carry viruses within their genes and it is possible that these viruses could combine to create entirely new organisms. The public are rightly concerned about the possible health and environmental consequences of the genetic engineering of plants for food: now xenotransplantation threatens the integrity of the human body itself.

All transplanted organs are liable to rejection—the body's own defence mechanism's attempt to destroy the "foreign" organ. To try to prevent this, the body's defences must be suppressed with large doses of very powerful and toxic immunosuppressant drugs.

Xenotransplants bring far more violent responses such as hyperacute rejection, an extremely strong reaction which destroys the new organ within minutes. It is thought that introducing human genes into pigs may avert this hyperacute response, but the pig organ will still face other rejection processes which scientists believe will be stronger than those faced by human organs. Finally, even if the pig organs survived there is strong evidence to suggest that they will fail to function adequately within the human body.

Some viruses carried by pigs are impossible to eradicate. Experiments have shown that these viruses can infect human tissue, and there have been many instances of diseases crossing between species with catastrophic results BSE/CJD,[1] HIV and the . . . chicken flu epidemic in Hong Kong. Not only does this threaten the people who would receive pig organs, but scientists the world over are concerned that these viruses may pass into the general population, causing an epidemic that could affect us all. Patients receiving xenotransplants will have to take immunosuppressants to prevent rejection—drugs that inhibit the very defences that protect us against such diseases.

> "Nothing could be worse than if in trying to save our lives we inadvertently engineered a plague." *New Scientist* Editorial 8th August 1998

Animals Are Being Abused

Xenotransplantation research is being conducted not by charities or universities, but by commercial pharmaceutical and biotechnology companies. The main UK researcher is owned by Novartis, a multinational drug company which also supplies the major anti-rejection drug Cyclosporin. One estimate suggests a potential market of US$6 billion for genetically manipulated animal organs, with $5 billion for sales of the associated drugs. Public health, and the lives and well-being of hundreds of thousands of animals are being jeopardised, ultimately, for the sake of profit.

Should xenotransplantation ever become a reality, pigs will be turned into spare part factories, plundered for their organs. Genetically-mutated and raised in artificial conditions, these remarkably intelligent animals face an unnatural and distressing existence. Other animals have been subjected to horrific experiments, including the grafting of hamster hearts into rabbits, and pig hearts into monkeys. Many of them have had to be destroyed soon after receiving the "foreign" organ because of their immense suffering.

These experiments can never tell us whether animal-to-human transplants will work. In a . . . European poll only 36% of people found xenotransplantation acceptable. A British poll found only 21% in favour, yet the Government are set to allow it to take place without even consulting Parliament. The risk of new viruses affects us all: we are taking part in an experiment against our will.

---

1. Bovine spongiform encephalopathy ("mad cow disease") and Creutzfeldt-Jakob disease are fatal brain diseases that can be acquired by eating diseased meat.

BSE shows us the dangers of meddling with nature. Nuclear weapons show us the dangers of unleashing forces which we cannot control.

A Perilous Future

Xenotransplantation is fraught with dangers known and unknown: our concern for those suffering from organ failure must not lead us to make a terrible and irreversible mistake.

"It is well established that most new emerging human infectious diseases generally have their origins in other species. A direct method of establishing new infectious human disease would be to implant infected tissues from a nonhuman species into humans thus allowing viruses direct access to human tissues. . . . Seldom, if ever, have we had as much knowledge to prevent a future epidemic. What is lacking is the wisdom to act upon that knowledge."

Dr Jon Allan, Virologist, Southwest Foundation
for Biomedical Research, Texas, USA.

"If we go ahead with xenotransplantation, it will be a step in the dark."

Professor Tony Minson, Virologist, Cambridge University.

"If you are putting your bets on containment, it's a lost cause. . . . It is odd that a small number of people in the government are making unilateral decisions about something that could have such long-term consequences for the public."

Dr Jon Allan.

"If you have a pig transplant, you may die of leukaemia in twenty years time."

Dr David White. Founder of Imutran Ltd., biotechnology
company at forefront of development of xenotransplantation.

"There are lots of viruses in pigs. One problem is that pigs have a kind of retrovirus (a retrovirus is the same family of viruses as HIV) which cannot be eliminated from the pig because it is inherited in the pig's own DNA yet can come out as an infectious virus. What we have shown is that up to three strains of pig retrovirus can propagate in human cells, in culture, therefore there is a risk that they could infect humans and might cause disease in humans."

Professor Robin Weiss, Virologist, Institute of
Cancer Research, London. 3rd November 1999.

Xenotransplantation Is Immoral

Before referring specifically to the Draft Report,[2] I would like to reiterate (Uncaged Campaigns's) overarching ethical position on the subject of xenotransplantation.

Uncaged Campaigns believes that xenotransplantation is intrinsically im-

---

2. A report issued by the Infection Surveillance Steering Group, part of the United Kingdom Xenotransplantation Interim Regulatory Authority, on the extent of and ways to avoid the risks of xenotransplantations.

moral in terms of its exploitation of nonhuman animals. Animals such as pigs (and humans, for that matter) have vital interests in avoiding deliberately-inflicted suffering, fulfilling their desires and instincts, and not being killed. Their incarceration, the frustration of their natural instincts as a result of their housing conditions, and their destruction all represent fundamental abuses of their moral right to have their vital interests respected.

The prospect of xenotransplantation threatens to extend our society's abuse of animals. Therefore it represents a retrograde step in the progress of our civilisation. We appear to becoming more barbaric and more violent. The goal of extending human life in the face of naturally-occurring disease does not justify the exploitation and killing of other animals, notwithstanding the potential costs of xenotransplantation to both human recipients and the wider population. Therefore, in our considered opinion, the entire exercise of drawing up systems for infection surveillance is premised upon a morally unjustifiable position: that xenotransplantation is acceptable.

> *"Should xenotransplantation ever become a reality, pigs will be turned into spare part factories."*

However, we are aware that the UKXIRA's [United Kingdom Xenotransplantation Interim Regulatory Authority] deliberations are supposed to be based upon the ethical conclusions of the Kennedy Report.[3] While we regard the moral positions adopted by the Kennedy Report as mistaken, illogical and arbitrary, we will suggest that the central conclusion one must inevitably draw from the Draft Report, taking into account the Kennedy moral framework, is that xenotransplantation should still not proceed.

This was the core ethical position adopted by the Kennedy Report:

> "We conclude that the use of the pig for xenotransplantation may be ethically acceptable. We conclude further, however, that the acceptability lies in balancing the benefit to humans against the harm both to the pig and to humans."
>
> [Recommendation 9, Para 4.30]

It is this "balancing" or cost/benefit process which is supposed to underpin the UKXIRA's on-going deliberations. We emphasise this point because some comments made by UKXIRA members lead us to fear that this ethical basis is being ignored.

The Draft Report of the Infection Surveillance Steering Group obviously has important implications for the cost/benefit analysis insofar as it indicates further potential costs to be borne by xenograft recipients and the wider population. It is our opinion that a complete and unbiased assessment of these costs will lead to the conclusion that the costs of xenotransplantation outweigh the benefits, and that therefore the xenotransplantation project should be aban-

---

3. The Kennedy Report was published by Britain's Department of Health's Advisory Group on the Ethics of Xenotransplantation in January 1997.

doned, to quote one of the options mentioned by Professor Herb Sewell at [1999's] Annual Meeting.

Health Risks Cannot Be Controlled

The key aim of the proposed surveillance system is to minimise the risk to public health from xenozoonoses through the rapid recognition and control of outbreaks.

Our first, broad observation is that controlling microbiological phenomena is an uncertain and risky affair in general. The risk posed by viruses, especially retroviruses, presents particular difficulties in terms of detection and treatment. The Kennedy report acknowledges:

> "Viruses are difficult to treat with drugs and can mutate rapidly to resist the immune system; thereby infecting humans more readily. . . . A further major problem lies in the inability to identify even known viruses. Infection with viruses can be difficult to detect. Even where the virus is known and a test has been developed, the test may be insensitive or give false positive results."

The problems of detection and treatment with unknown viruses are even more unfathomable. It is generally acknowledged that unknown porcine viruses exist.

Recipients of xenografts will be quite ill in the first place, and the administration of immunosuppressant drugs is likely to increase the range of symptoms they experience. In these circumstances, it will be difficult to identify a particular symptom as being the result of a xenozoonosis, further compounding the inherent complications of detection.

The limits of knowledge were exemplified by the recently announced results of tests on the tissue of a baboon liver recipient who was found to have been infected with a virus from the animal seven years after they had died. It had been thought that the herpes virus that had infected him was incapable of infecting humans. The fact that this incident involved a primate and not a pig should not be used as an excuse for complacency for it demonstrates the unpredictability and mysteriousness of viruses in general.

The . . . "Nipah" virus outbreak in Malaysia is an extremely worrying event in terms of its implications for the safety of xenotransplantation. The virus, which passed from pigs to humans, had never been seen before, and killed over a hundred of the two hundred and fifty or so people it infected.

Currently, the main virus of concern is the porcine endogenous retrovirus (PERV). One particularly worrying aspect of PERVs is that they may infect a recipient and then remain latent for many years. Even if a retroviral infection could be identified after it emerged after several years, it may be too late to stop the virus from spreading around the general population. If symptoms emerged initially in a non-recipient (because the original recipient had died before they had showed symptoms or the virus had been detected, for example), identifying the source of the outbreak as a xenotransplant would be even more difficult.

Confident assertions of "control" over microbiological phenomena, particularly viruses and retroviruses, are dangerously deluded, in our opinion. To quote Dr Jon Allan: "If you're putting your bets on containment, it's a lost cause."

A Burden to Recipients

Apart from the intrinsic difficulties with attempts to survey and control infections, there are a number of additional practical difficulties with the draft proposals.

Many recent newspaper headlines have focussed on the proposal to require xenograft recipients to abstain from having children. This is perhaps the least one would expect from such recipients, and it is probably the easiest requirement to monitor, relative to other requirements. Obviously though, the patients who perhaps have most to gain from a xenograft—younger recipients—would have most to lose from a subsequent ban on reproduction. In the case of young male recipients, ensuring that they do not father any children will be particularly problematic.

The stipulation that recipients must agree to use barrier contraception consistently and for life will be very difficult to enforce in practice. With the best will in the world, it will be inevitable that some recipients will fail to comply with this requirement "consistently and for life".

Questions of consent and enforcement become even more difficult and dubious around the requirement for recipients to have their current and future sexual partners registered and monitored by health authorities. In particular, is it really ethical and practical to expect future sexual partners to be bound by arrangements made by their partners before their relationship started? We think not.

The lifelong monitoring system for recipients envisages a testing frequency of once a year after one year, with the frequency of sampling reviewed after two years. Given the possibility of any xenozoonotic infection remaining latent before emerging after a number of years, the proposed sampling frequencies appear to be inadequate. The practical difficulties of ensuring that recipients comply with these requirements several years after transplantation are also worrying. There will inevitably be a tendency towards complacency in this situation.

Ironically, should xenotransplantation become fairly effective (though we believe this is unlikely, especially in the case of organs), this will proportionately increase the difficulties in ensuring lifetime monitoring of recipients.

If no "untoward events" appeared in initial small-scale clinical trials, then the Steering Group envisages a relaxation of the surveillance programme. Indeed, such a relaxation "would

> *"Xenotransplantation is intrinsically immoral in terms of its exploitation of nonhuman animals."*

have to be the case before xenotransplantation could be used [in] a routine therapy." (The Draft Report does not explain why this would be the case.) We firmly believe that any proposals to relax surveillance requirements would lead to public health being jeopardised to an even greater extent. Given that the risk of xenozoonosis is acknowledged to be small, the likelihood of an untoward event occurring is likely to increase in proportion with the numbers and survival rates of any recipients. To propose to relax surveillance requirements under such circumstances is illogical and dangerous in the extreme. The potential for any infection to remain latent exacerbates the long-term hazard of xenozoonosis.

The proposed post-xenotransplantation surveillance scheme for contacts is disturbingly inadequate. Once again, the potential for latent infection underlines the need for consistent monitoring for life. The current scheme is far too reactive, relying as it does on the identification of xenozoonotic "untoward events". Reacting to infections that may cause symptoms after being latent is like shutting the stable door once the horse has bolted. In such cases, the so-called "incident control team" will be superfluous.

> *"One must strongly question whether it is possible . . . for potential recipients to really give the matter cool, rational consideration."*

Aside from doubts over effectiveness, the prospect of introducing rapid emergency legislation, including detention for testing, in the event of a xenozoonotic outbreak threatens to breach basic human rights to liberty. Although prospective recipients in a life and death situation may agree to submit to such measures in the instance of an "untoward event" (although problems will arise regarding how valid consent could be obtained in such circumstances), imposing such restrictions on contacts and partners could be extremely problematic.

Issues of Consent

Transplant patients who are being asked to agree to these measures are going to be in a fairly desperate situation. We acknowledge the emphasis that the Draft Report places on the need for extensive and unbiased information to be supplied to potential recipients. However, we are sceptical as to whether information provided to such patients would really be objective. Although the UKXIRA could check on materials intended for presentation to the patient, subtle underlying biases and pressures are bound to creep into the interactions between the prospective patient and the "independent" information-giver. (We have placed the word "independent" in quotes because we feel that such a person, with the best will in the world will have underlying prejudices in favour of xenotransplantation, or will feel indirect pressure from xenotransplantation teams to bring about a positive response to proposals to conduct xenotransplantation.)

Additionally, one must strongly question whether it is possible, in such a situation, for potential recipients to really give the matter cool, rational consideration: therefore it is debatable whether valid consent is possible.

Given the risks posed to society in general by xenozoonosis, for xenotransplantation to fulfil just one of the necessary ethical conditions, some satisfactory mechanism for democratic assent to xenotransplantation procedures must be obtained. Although approaches to this question are beyond the scope of the Draft report, such issues are central to the overall ethical acceptability of xeno-transplantation. We believe that such issues have not been adequately addressed by the UKXIRA or the Government.

The infection surveillance scheme outlined by the Steering Group in the Draft Report is designed to minimise the risk not only to recipients and contacts who may have actively consented to surveillance requirements, but also to society in general. It is this risk to the general public which poses particular ethical, legal and practical problems. Given this universally acknowledged risk to society, one would expect that society, acting through the instrument of government, should be able to enforce the necessary measures to protect itself. The conclusion, therefore, that society cannot act collectively to try to protect itself through a surveillance scheme, raises, in our view, further insurmountable ethical obstacles to xenotransplantation. Relying on voluntary consent to compliance is not only unsafe, but removes the right of society as a whole to defend itself.

The practical reasons why we believe voluntary consent to be an inadequate safeguard can be summarised as follows:

> The lifelong compliance and numerous additional conditions . . . are complex, demanding and certainly vulnerable to human error. It would not be credible to expect all patients to comply with all these conditions, even with the best will in the world. Indeed, the Draft Report acknowledges this when it admits that legislation will "probably" not be needed, and that patients will "normally" perceive the need to attend regular check-ups.

> Patients will be aware that they retain the right to withdraw from post-operative surveillance schemes at any time.

> In practice, expecting recipient's contacts to comply with surveillance requirements will be even more difficult. Changes in patients' future relationships will complicate this situation further. Although the Group suggests: "Patients may need to be counselled about telling future sexual partners about their status as xenotransplant recipients," this cannot go anywhere near far enough to give us confidence that all such contacts would submit to the necessary requirements.

> The higher the degree of success for xenografts, the more likely it will be that recipients and contacts will fail to comply with life-time monitoring and other conditions.

The Social Costs Are Too High

A lack of confidence in voluntary consent leads us to conclude that xeno-transplantation does indeed give rise to a public interest justification for the introduction of legislation to ensure compliance with surveillance requirements.

Having said that, the Steering Group's conclusion is understandable in the light of the serious potential breaches of human rights that would be contained in legislation to "protect" public health from xenozoonoses. Therefore, the controversy over the question of whether to introduce legislation to enforce surveillance requirements brings sharply into focus the significant and serious social dangers posed by xenotransplantation, and the practical difficulties inherent in attempts to minimise the risk to public health. If it is unethical and impractical to enforce, through legislation, the (inadequate, in our view) surveillance requirements necessary to try to minimise the danger posed to society in general by xenotransplantation, then we must acknowledge that xenotransplantation is unethical, purely in terms of its social costs.

Creating a Market for the Sale of Organs Is Ethical

by Curtis E. Harris and Stephen P. Alcorn

About the authors: *Curtis E. Harris is a physician and an associate clinical professor at the University of Oklahoma School of Medicine. Stephen P. Alcorn is an assistant district attorney in Oklahoma County, Oklahoma.*

Currently, 68,000 Americans are waiting for an organ donation, with a name added to the list every sixteen minutes. Twelve Americans die every day because a needed vital organ is not available. The congressional answer has been the Uniform Anatomical Gift Act, which was designed to promote public awareness, health care provider education, and to prohibit the sale of most human organs.

Where gaps in the law prohibiting the sale of human tissue have been left allowed, a thriving market exists, meeting the needs of Americans for blood, tissue, and human reproductive cells. However, vital organs are prohibited from sale.

Proposals have been made over the years to adopt free market principles to the open sale of organs, allowing vital organs to be bought and sold for whatever price the market could sustain. The potential for abuse in a system such as this is real and has always prevented the serious consideration of such an open market.

This article proposes a governmentally regulated, posthumous organ market in which licensed brokerage houses operate under the oversight of the Food and Drug Administration. Though regulated, flexibility will be necessary to allow the laws of supply-and-demand to control most aspects of the market. Through this combination of regulation and a free market, needless loss of life can be prevented and equity in organ distribution maintained. . . .

Altruism Has Failed

The United States has always relied upon altruism for organ procurement. While this system leaves the decision to the individual and preserves personal autonomy, it does so at the expense of effective organ procurement. Though Congress and the States continue to tinker with various forms of both awareness and encouragement, few programs have proven to be effective. A noteworthy exception has been Pennsylvania's *Organ Donation Trust Fund*, established by statute in 1994. The trust fund authorizes the state to pay up to $3,000 to the donor's hospital or funeral home to cover donor associated expenses. Even though no payments have yet been made, the program has been remarkably successful: three million Pennsylvanians have signed up to donate organs and citizens have donated nearly a million dollars to the trust fund. This is a remarkable achievement, and if even a small percentage of registered donors actually follow through with an organ donation, it will make a real difference. This success can be compared with Virginia, which only had approximately 180,000 potential donors registered with the Department of Motor Vehicles in 1998.

The federal government has yet to take any bold or innovative steps to increase organ donation, and what has been done thus far has arguably been worse than doing nothing. Time and effort has been spent in disputes over distribution of existing organs rather than finding new organ donors. The altruistic system in the United States has fallen short, failing badly to close the gap between organ donation and organ need. The various versions of the Anatomical Gift Act have produced no real change in the number of available organs.

Between 1989 and 1992 the demand for organs increased 66%, while donations during that same period increased 33%. During those years, 10,000 people died while waiting for an organ transplant.

The number of transplant operations continues to rise every year. In 1998, 20,861 transplants were performed, but the need for transplants continues to outpace supply. As of March 2000, 68,371 were on the waiting list to receive an organ.

With great fanfare, the Department of Health and Human Services (HHS) announced that in 1998 organ donation increased 5.6%, the first substantial increase in three years. Yet HHS admits demand increased that year by almost 14%. To meet this demand, HHS proposed a new campaign designed to increase donation 20% over two years. If adopted, the program would focus on three areas HHS has determined to be key: public awareness, health care provider education, and legislative initiatives.

"The federal government has yet to take any bold or innovative steps to increase organ donation."

Even assuming that this program succeeds in achieving its 20% goal, there will still be 41,993 people on the waiting list in need of an organ. The inadequacy of the HHS plan is even more apparent if demand continues to rise at a 14% rate: 53,751 people will be without a vital organ by the end of the year 2000. Currently, a new name is added to the national waiting list every sixteen minutes.

By any calculation the need for organs has become critical. The government continues to propose solutions that have previously failed to provide an answer. While HHS continues to insist that altruism will work, twelve Americans are dying every day. It is time for a fundamental change in the system.

Fears and Myths

Objections to an open market approach to organ procurement generally fall into four basic categories: fear and urban myth, concern over unhealthy organs, objections to the trade in human flesh, and the overall availability of organs.

Much of the fear and urban myth is encouraged by the entertainment industry. Popular shows such as *Walker, Texas Ranger*, and *Law and Order*, portray organ snatching criminals. *Coma*, the popular book and movie written by Robin Cook, tells the story of a criminal gang that abducts young people to provide organs for wealthy individuals. Books, movies and television tap into our fear, and distort both facts and the capabilities of science and physiology.

Fanciful entertainment has made a population fearful to even consider an open organ market. Urban myths invariably include stories, told by an uncle or cousin, who knew someone whose friend had been on a business trip and remembers blacking out in a bar after only a drink or two. The unfortunate business traveler awoke in a tub of ice with staples in his back and a kidney removed.

"A system that protects against abuses but encourages donors must be found."

History has also fueled the fear of an organ market. English medical schools during the 19th Century purchased cadavers at eleven times the average worker's weekly salary. By the 1820s "resurrectionists" were snatching bodies from cemeteries throughout the country. The practice eventually led to the actions of the notorious Burke and Hare, who lured derelicts into their Edinburgh apartment with the promise of a fine local malt, only to murder and then sell them to a medical school. Today Scottish tour guides still relish the squirms and gasps of tourists when they recount the story in front of the infamous apartment.

A similar reaction occurred in the United States when reports of an *E-Bay* auction of a kidney were widely published. On September 2, 1999, a healthy man auctioned his kidney on the World Wide Web. Bidding started at $25,000 and had reached $5,750,100 by the time website administrators halted the process. Though assumed by most to be a joke, it received general public condemnation.

Poorly grounded public opinion aside, there are several valid and thoughtful concerns regarding the open organ market. One concern is that the market will be flooded with unhealthy organs. It is assumed that poor, malnourished individuals will sell their organs out of desperation, or that drug abusers and alcoholics will sell organs to get money to continue their habits.

Issues of equity and human dignity are also of concern. Will the poor in third world countries be lured by exaggerated fees and promises? Will governments begin to look at prisoners as an economic resource, as China has? Is it immoral to economically entice the poor to submit to dangerous procedures so that the wealthy can continue physically punishing lifestyles? Is the human body really a commodity, and if so, what does this say to our strong opposition to slavery and the economic exploitation of children and women worldwide? Finally, if a market system exits, will anyone voluntarily donate? This could mean that only the wealthy would have a chance to receive a costly organ.

Live Donor Markets

Organ markets have been proposed using both live and posthumous donors. In a living market system, individuals would be allowed to sell non-vital organs, such as a kidney, part of a liver, and possibly a lung. This right-of-sale would place non-vital organs in a similar category as is currently held by blood, sperm, oocytes, and body tissue—all of which are legally sold.

A live donor market is not an entirely foreign concept to Americans. [In 2000] 4,017 living donors gave kidneys to relatives, friends, or acquaintances. These donations accounted for almost 31% of all kidneys transplanted. Between January and September of 1999, one hundred live donors gave part of their livers.

There are even two cases reported in 1999 in which individuals made an undirected donation of a kidney. This allowed the medical centers involved to accurately choose the appropriate candidate for the organ, even though the patient was a stranger to the donor.

Proponents of a live donor market are convinced that even more donors would step forward if given a certain kind of nudge: that is, an economic incentive.

Existing Parallels

One need look no further than oocyte donation to see an example of market theory applied to organ procurement. First, it is important to realize oocyte donation is complex and clearly invasive. Oocyte extraction starts with a three week treatment of a hormone called Lupron. This drug completely halts ovulation for a month. The donor then injects Pergonal and Metrodin (follicle stimulating hormones) into her buttocks every morning for eight days. This forces ovarian hyperfunction, causing engorgement of the ovaries and rapid oocyte development. After the eighth day the donor receives a final shot of a hormone, Human Chronic Gonadotropin. Exactly thirty-six hours later, she is put under general sedation. An ultrasound probe is inserted into the donor's vagina and a needle is then inserted into each ovary extracting twelve oocytes, one at a time. Therefore, in both complexity and risk, oocyte donation parallels organ donation in several regards.

Recently an advertisement seeking oocyte donors appeared in an Ivy League newspaper. The first week two hundred women responded and in the second, one hundred. Though ooctye donation was first done in 1984, it is predicted that 5,000 women will donate this year. What drives these young women to become donors despite the obvious risk and discomfort? Money. They receive between $4,000 to $35,000 per donation. Proponents of a living donor organ market feel that they can be equally successful.

Objections to a Living Donor Market

Exploitation of the poor is the most frequent objection to a living donor organ market. The concern is that some people may see the sale of their organs as the only solution to their economic hardship.

Opponents of an organ market point to the current trend of ooctye donation: most are from students at private colleges who are receiving little financial help from family. These women see donation as their only way to cope with the rising costs of a quality education. Thus, a logical question arises: Do we want to live in an America where, in order to receive a quality education, one must sell a body part, an oocyte . . . or a kidney?

A world-wide black market is also a concern. In 1989 the World Health Organization passed a resolution condemning the sale of human organs for transplant purposes based on documented abuses in poor nations. The 1980s saw a growing black market for organ sales in the Middle East. In 1991 a 35-year-old Egyptian man sold his kidney because he was poor and had no prospect of work. He simply decided to sell what he had left to sell—his body.

Finally, the real example of China's sale of organs from executed prisoners and the fear that the practice may become more common is enough to give anyone pause. A system that protects against abuses but encourages donors must be found.

Some Regulation Is Necessary

A free market in organs was a serious reality in 1983 when a Virginia man, H. Barry Jacobs, founded International Kidney Exchange Ltd. His company proposed to act as a broker, representing those in need of an organ and finding those willing to sell. Jacobs offered to pay up to $10,000 for a healthy kidney, and the purchaser would pay for the cost of the kidney, all related expenses, and a brokerage fee of $2,000–5,000 per kidney.

Jacobs intended not only to recruit sellers in America, but also look to Third World sources as well. Acknowledging that informed consent from illiterates would be difficult, he planned to video tape consent.

Six months after Jacobs announced his intentions, the State of Virginia banned the sale of organs. Shortly thereafter the U.S. Congress took similar steps. The Jacobs experiment in a *completely* free market with no government control or guidance was disturbing. It was the extreme in organ procurement and the very situation critics of an organ market system feared.

But a market in organs need not, in fact should not, be entirely free or open. There are few if any areas of the American economy that do not have some government regulation or control, especially if the market is significant. If the market in organs were a controlled market, akin to the radio and television industry, it is likely that organ shortages could be addressed without the objections and fears mentioned earlier. Direct and indirect financial

> *"A market in organs need not, in fact should not, be entirely free or open."*

encouragement can be structured to avoid abuses, and to reserve altruism as a central motive.

In light of the problems and concerns noted above, we propose the following plan to partially regulate a market in organs and expand the rights of donors. First, we believe that a posthumous market would be the most widely supported of the market systems, chiefly because it addresses the major concerns raised by opponents of a living donor market. To function well, this system must establish a statutory right to dispose of one's organs; and it must allow a contractual agreement for monies to be paid to the donor's estate upon death and the retrieval of fit organs. Further, the contract should be based on performance and not on a promise, allowing the donor, but not the family, to revoke the contract at any time.

Payment would only be made for those organs that were fit. A medical center would not have to pay for a liver that was, subsequent to the contract, destroyed by alcohol or incident to the donor's death.

Preventing Abuses

Inasmuch as the donor would never himself receive the money, it would decrease the likelihood of organ sales encouraged by drug abuse or situational depression. This approach would also reduce, though not eliminate, the likelihood of the potential abuse of the poor and other vulnerable groups since the sale of organs would be effective only upon the death of the donor.

The decedent's relatives would be prohibited from selling his organs without the prior consent of the decedent, and this consent could only take the form of a valid contract—thus allowing for control of one's body even after death.

Other safeguards should be added to this system. Prior to entering into this contract the donor would be required to undergo a screening process which would include a mental health assessment. This screening would ideally ascertain any hidden motives as to donation or mental instability at the time of the decision, and establish informed consent.

No minor would be allowed to contract, nor would parents be allowed to enter their child into a contract. This would alleviate fears of children being conceived solely for the purpose of growing organs.

As in insurance policies, an organ market would have "slayer provisions" as well as suicide clauses. If a third party beneficiary murdered the donor, he would not be allowed to be unjustly enriched by this criminal act. Nor would a contract be valid in the case of suicide, thus eliminating the concern of contracting for the betterment of his family's immediate needs.

Intriguing contractual arrangements could be driven by the market. There may be a "Healthy Life Style" bonus. Runners may receive a higher contracting price than those with a sedentary lifestyle. Non-smokers and people at their ideal height and weight may receive a financial bonus. These items and benefits could be driven by supply and demand of the market.

A completely free market would invite the kind of abuse that so far has doomed any serious consideration of an organ market. In this area governmental regulation would not only be beneficial but would also be crucial. The Food and Drug Administration would be a logical candidate to oversee an organ market. Through the FDA the government can address the concerns of a trade in organs while allowing the country to benefit from an increased supply.

The FDA could issue a limited number of licenses to private companies that would serve as brokerage houses. The cost of governmental oversight would be subsidized by licensing fees. These fees could also be used to develop altruistic donation programs as well as transplant opportunities for the under and uninsured. The FDA could choose to impose a flat per organ donation rate but would need to provide for market driven price fluctuations.

Currently 68,371 Americans are on waiting lists to receive an organ. Twelve will die each day because there is no transplant organ available. Altruistic donations of organs have increased, but donations lag far behind the increase in demand. A creative solution to the shortage of donated organs should include the controlled posthumous free market sale of organs. It is time we learn from the successes of the plasma and reproductive cell markets and implement a well conceived, governmentally regulated posthumous organ market.

Creating a Market for the Sale of Organs Is Not Ethical

by James F. Childress

About the author: *James F. Childress is the director of the Institute of Practical Ethics at the University of Virginia, where he also teaches religious and biomedical ethics.*

The number of patients awaiting an organ transplant exceeded 75,000 in late March [2001]. Yet in 1999, the last year for which there are complete figures, there only were 21,655 transplants with organs from 4,717 living donors and 5,859 from cadavers (many of which provided more than one organ). Organ donation continues to fall further and further behind the demand for organs, and new initiatives have failed to reduce the gap. In this situation, why shouldn't we turn to the free market to increase the supply of transplantable organs, which can save lives and improve the quality of life?

Buying or selling an organ isn't always morally wrong. We don't, and shouldn't, always condemn those who sell or purchase an organ. We can understand why someone might do so. But should we change our laws to permit sales of organs and even enforce contracts to sell organs? Should we turn away from a system of gifts to a market in organs?

Arguments Against Selling Organs

Our society has very strong reasons not to allow the transfer of organs from the living or the dead for money. In presenting these reasons, it is useful to separate the acquisition of organs from their distribution. Normally, acquisition and distribution go together. However, if those who need organs had to purchase them directly, then the poor would end up selling organs to the rich—a distribution that would strike many as unfair. Thus, let's assume that the government or a private organization under government regulation will purchase organs and then distribute them in a fair and equitable way. I'll call this an "organ-procurement market."

Such a market could target living donors or cadaveric sources of organs. I use the term "sources" because those who sell their organs are not donors, they are sellers or vendors. Let's begin with cadaveric organs removed after an individual's death.

The main argument for rescinding the federal prohibition on the sale of organs is based on utility—allowing the sale of organs would increase their supply. But would a market actually increase the number of cadaveric organs for transplantation? Despite the claims of market fundamentalists, we simply do not know whether a market would reduce the scarcity of organs, in contrast to many other goods. And we have good reasons to be skeptical.

Indeed, I will argue, we shouldn't legalize a market in organ procurement because it probably would be ineffective, perhaps counterproductive (in reducing donations and possibly even the overall number of organs available for transplantation) and likely change our attitudes and practices by commodifying the human body and its parts. Furthermore, it is unnecessary to take this route, with all its problems, because we can make the system of donation effective without such ethical risks.

Not an Effective Alternative

It would be unwise to move away from a system of donation unless we have good evidence that a market actually would increase the supply of organs. After all, organ donations provide a substantial (though insufficient) number of organs. Some evidence against a potential market's effectiveness in cadaveric organ procurement comes from the reasons people now give for not signing donor cards. One proponent of the market contends that people now fail to donate "because of inertia, mild doubts about their preferences, a slight distaste for considering the subject or the inconvenience involved in completing or carrying a donor card." If these reasons for nondonation were the only ones, a market in cadaveric organ procurement probably would work. In fact, however, opinion polls indicate that fears of being declared dead prematurely or having one's death hastened in order to provide organs seriously inhibit many from signing donor cards.

The fears and distrust that limit organ donation would render utterly ineffective a system of organ procurement based on sales. A futures market—whereby individuals contract now for delivery of organs upon their deaths—is the most defensible because people sell their own, not others', organs. However, if people at present are reluctant to sign donor cards because they fear they may not receive proper care in the hospital, imagine their fears about accepting money for the delivery of usable organs upon their deaths. Once they have signed the contract, all that remains for its fulfillment is their death. And a regulated market would not eliminate their fears. After all, such fears persist in our regulated system of organ donation.

Critics often contend that allowing sales of organs would turn bodies and parts into commodities. Such commodification could lead us to think about and treat dead bodies in merely instrumental terms, thereby damaging important social values. In addition, many claim, commodification could damage and even reduce altruism. A market in organs would drive out, or very substantially reduce, organ donations, in part because it would redefine acts of donating organs. No longer would donors provide the "gift of life"—they instead would donate the equivalent of the market value of the organs provided.

> *"The assertion of a moral right to sell a kidney against the legal prohibition of such a sale is not persuasive."*

In short, market defenders have not proposed an effective system to obtain additional cadaveric organs. Not only would a procurement market probably be ineffective, it could be counterproductive and have other social costs. Its financial costs would not be negligible. Furthermore, the system of donation has features, including its connection with altruism, that make it ethically preferable, other things being equal. And we can make our system of express donation more effective.

Current Programs Have Worked

It works fairly well now. For example, according to some estimates, the acts of cadaveric-organ donation in 1999 represented close to half of the patients who died in circumstances where their organs could be salvaged for transplantation (usually following brain death). It might be possible, and desirable, to expand the categories of potential donors to include many who die according to cardiopulmonary standards. Beyond expanding the criteria of donor eligibility, we need to work to make effective the recently adopted policy of required referral. This policy mandates referral to an organ-procurement organization that can then ask the family about organ donation.

Programs to educate the public about organ donation must attend to attitudes of distrust and mistrust, not merely to the tremendous need for organs. It is difficult to alter those attitudes, but increasing the public's understanding of brain death certainly is one way to proceed.

The public's willingness to donate cadaveric organs generally presupposes trust not only in the society's criteria and procedures for determining death, but in its criteria for fairly and effectively distributing donated organs as well. In addition, the provision of access to basic health care for everyone would create a sense of solidarity that dramatically could increase organ donation, but that vision is a distant one.

I salute the decisions in some states to give the decedent's signed donor card priority over family objections, but it is even more important to educate individuals as members of families. They need to share their decisions with their families and consider their roles as potential donors of a family member's organs. Donor cards may be a useful mechanism to stimulate such conversations, but in and of themselves they are too individualistic, legalistic and formalistic. The process of intrafamilial communication is more important.

Society also provides various incentives for organ donation, such as by recognizing and honoring donors in various ways. Would it be possible to offer some financial incentives without crossing over into a market for organ procurement? Consider the following: As a regular expression of its gratitude for organ donation, society could cover the decedent's funeral expenses up to a certain amount, perhaps $1,000 or more. In this way, the community would recognize with gratitude the decedent's and/or the family's act of donation and also pay respects to the donor or source of the organs by sharing in the disposition of his/her final remains.

Any proposal for such "rewarded gifting" will require careful scrutiny, in part because organ donation is such a highly sensitive area, marked by complex beliefs, symbols, attitudes, sentiments and practices, some of them religious in nature. But a carefully conceived pilot experiment, such as providing death benefits—as Pennsylvania has discussed—may be justifiable. However, it may infringe current laws. In any event, it requires the utmost caution because of its risks. One risk is that it will be perceived as purchasing organs rather than as incentives for donation.

The Risks of a Living Organ Market

I have focused on cadaveric organs, but what about a market in organ procurement from living individuals? Such a market probably would be more effective than a futures market in cadaveric organs—more individuals probably would be willing to part with a kidney, especially with reduced risks from kidney removal and with generous compensation. However, the social risk of commodification—of treating living human bodies and their parts as commodities—is very troubling. In addition, the risks of coercion and exploitation, especially of poor people, are substantial. The assertion of a moral right to sell a kidney against the legal prohibition of such a sale is not persuasive; we have good reasons, based on concerns about commodification, coercion and exploitation, to reject such sales as incompatible with our moral vision of the kind of society to which we aspire.

Vigorous efforts along the paths I have indicated should obviate the need to adopt a market in organ procurement, whether from living or cadaveric sources. We have little reason to believe that a futures market will be effective in obtaining cadaveric organs and considerable reason to worry about the risks and social costs of such a market, as well as a market for living organ procurement. We should just say "no" to both markets.

Consent for Cadaver Organ Donation Is Unnecessary

by H.E. Emson

About the author: *H.E. Emson is a forensic pathologist.*

In my opinion any concept of property in the human body either during life or after death is biologically inaccurate and morally wrong. The body should be regarded as on loan to the individual from the biomass, to which the cadaver will inevitably return. Development of immunosuppressive drugs has resulted in the cadaver becoming a unique and invaluable resource to those who will benefit from organ donation. Faced with the biological reality, the moral error of any concept of property in the body, and the quantitative failure of voluntary organ donation, I believe that the right of control over the cadaver should be vested in the state as representative of those who may benefit from organ donation.

Defining Cadavers

How one regards the dead human body, the cadaver, is in part governed by one's familiarity with it. At the present time, very few people ever see a cadaver which has not in some way been altered after death, and even fewer touch, handle, deal in any way with the dead human body. In developed countries, death itself most frequently occurs away from the home, in an institution, under the supervision of professional caregivers. For most people, ideas concerning the cadaver, its nature, the proper way to deal with it, are formed under these conditions.

As a pathologist specialising in forensic pathology, for 50 years I have been at the other end of the spectrum of experience. In my daily work I have been privileged to examine the cadaver in all its stages after death from the immediate postmortem moments through all the stages of decomposition to bare bones. Working in a relatively small community, I have sometimes been charged with examining the body of someone I have known in life, which is never an easy task. These experiences have moulded my ideas as to what the cadaver is, what it represents, and how it should be treated. My beliefs are by no means unique, but I believe the experience which has formed them is unusual and because of this, important. Reading the works of ethicists who pronounce upon these matters, I wonder how many of them have ever viewed and touched a human cadaver, or seen a decomposing body.

Out of all this I have become what I understand is termed a dichotomist, one who believes that the body and soul are separate, different entities. I use the term "soul" for want of a better, not knowing a word which does not in some way carry implications of the soul's origin, nature, value, and destination. I wish to imply none of these, nor to intrude here my own religious beliefs. For the purposes of this discussion, the soul to me is a non-physical, immaterial entity which animates the body and gives it what we know as life. In knowing and experiencing a person,

> *"The cadaver is not, what the body has been."*

we cannot separate body and soul, because we always know them together. From the moment of birth until that of death they are inseparable and intertwined to form the person, the human being. At death the soul departs from the body—I have watched this occur—and here I express no beliefs whatsoever as to what happens to it at that point; where it goes, if anywhere, what its future is, if any. What is clear to me is, that without the soul, the body is not and can never again be a part of the person. The cadaver is not, what the body has been.

The body, on the other hand, is more easily defined and described. This, the physical entity animated by the soul, is formed of chemical elements and compounds, organised into tissues and organs, combined in a marvellous complexity and with the soul, it is the human person. In this combined state, the person is alive; without the soul, the body is dead, with all that implies. From the moment of conception the component parts of the body are formed from material drawn from the external physical world, in active interchange and dynamic equilibrium with the biomass, the sum total of living organisms on the planet, and with some of its inorganic matter. We study the human person from its earliest beginnings, through growth, differentiation, maturity, decline, disease, and death. The life of the metazoan animal Homo sapiens, as we know it—and this is only one of the ways of considering the human being—is finite; senescence starts with the zygote, and corporeal death is its inevitable end.

Death and Decay

After death the human body decays, a process with which few are familiar and which excites revulsion which is both instinctive and learned. The instinctive part of this revulsion I think is easily explained, as an inherited reflex acquired by ancestral experience that rotten meat is not good to eat. Embedded very deeply in the nature of humanity there is another element to this, a belief that death is not the end of the soul and that the life of the body can somehow persist or be restored. This was expressed in the burial practices of the earliest humans, in the staining of bones of the deceased with red pigment as a symbol of continuing or resurgent life. Such practices have been elaborated by many different cultures, as in preservation and veneration of the bones of ancestors; burial with grave goods, food, slaughtered animals, and slaves, and mummification and embalming, to retain a simulacrum of continuing life, the last a common practice in many contemporary societies including our own. All these seek in some manner to deny the fact of death, or at the very least to delay its acceptance, to spread this as a process over a period of time, and to come to admit it gradually rather than as an instant blow at a single temporal point. Such practices often contrast oddly an expressed belief in an afterlife in a better world, with profound reluctance to leave this one. Many religions express belief in some form of "the resurrection of the body" but so far as I am aware, at the present time, this is only rarely interpreted as a strict physical reconstitution of its elements as at the moment of death. There is too much practical human experience for this, and however belief in a resurrection is interpreted, an element of symbolism is for most people inescapable.

However acceptance of death is denied or delayed, the human body is inexorably destined to decay as the beginning of a recycling process. Its constituent components are broken down by various means into simpler forms, and these in turn are recycled into the bodies of later generations of living things. We die and decay—or are burned—to come up again as wheat or roses, which in turn may form the bodies of future generations of people. Were this not so I would not be alive to write this, nor you to read it; the elements which might have formed us would all have been locked up in the indestructible physical remains of the first generation of living organisms. Decay is the inevitable and necessary consequence of finite corporeal mortal life.

Viewed from this point, the human body can only legitimately be regarded as on extended loan from the biomass, to the individual of which it forms a part, and any view of it as property which can be owned and disposed of must be examined very seriously, questioned, and modified. Our culture accepts as a fundamental principle that while the body is animated by the

> *"The body should be regarded morally as on loan from the biomass."*

soul, the person resulting from this union has a right to the preserved integrity of the body which is a necessary part of his or her total being. This is expressed in law, in our society, by prohibitions against killing, wounding, or even such minimal assault as threatening to touch the body without the person's consent. But how we should view the cadaver after death is a very different and much more questionable matter. In that part of the ethics of our society which is expressed in law, there is no concept of the cadaver as property which may be disposed of for gain. The law, formed over a period of time before the possibility of transplantation existed, at present charges someone with the responsibility to dispose of the cadaver in accordance with society's customary practice and the requirements of public health, and gives this person powers to do so, but the cadaver is not his or her property.

Cadavers Are Important Resources

Until very recently there was no significant value in a human cadaver, and no legitimate use for it save its quantitatively very minor utilisation in dissection as a part of the training of physicians and surgeons. All this changed, recently, suddenly and dramatically, with the invention of immunosuppressive drugs which block the bodily rejection of transplanted organs and tissues, and make organ transplantation possible as a practical and effective treatment of human disease. The change is tremendous, unprecedented, unparalleled in our experience. The difference—for example, between chronic haemodialysis and kidney transplantation for the treatment of renal failure, is the difference between existence and life. From the strictly practical viewpoint, from being an object without intrinsic value destined only for disposal, the cadaver became at one leap a vital resource, something quite new in human experience. This quantum jump in technological capability brought with it, as all such advances inevitably do, totally new ethical problems. These in their turn can and must be tackled, and possibly solved, and faced with the unprecedented, it can only be done by fundamental examination of our basic beliefs, and their reconciliation with immutable physical facts.

One thing which must be considered at the very beginning, is the problem of immediacy. To be effective, an organ for transplantation must be removed as soon after death as possible. But it may be very difficult for relatives to accept that their loved one's body, maintained in a semblence of life by artificial respiration, is in fact dead and will obviously be so when the respirator is turned off. Added to this, there is acceptance of death as a process, not as an event; a fact which those close to the deceased come to accept gradually and which in its fullness may take years. Some progress towards reconciling these facts—for human emotions are facts with which we must deal—and resolving this dilemma, can be made when the death of an individual is known to be inevitable but can be postponed for a short time during which the family can come to terms with it. A great deal more could be done by the more gradual and diffuse processes of public education, but while the problem can be lessened, it inevitably will remain. The cadaver has now become, to those who may receive its organs as replacement for their own which have failed, quite literally a source of continued life restored to something close to its fullness, and qualitatively different from existence maintained by mechanical means. In discussing this I shall limit myself to kidney transplantation, the commonest procedure which has become routine. Again, one wonders if some of the ethicists who pronounce on this, have ever met with and talked to patients who have experienced both existence maintained by haemodialysis, and life restored by transplantation. There is this real difference. This situation requires re-examination of basic beliefs; to whom does the cadaver "belong", and who should morally have rights to determine its disposal? To the deceased, it is something that has been a vital component of the person but now is no longer and is no more needed. To the bereaved family, it is a remaining part of the beloved deceased person, emotionally tremendously evocative, hallowed by individual experience and by centuries of belief and tradition. To the potential recipient of its donated organs, it is the very new hope of restored life.

Bodies Cannot Be Owned

I do not think that the concept of ownership or property in the human body is an accurate, defensible, or moral one, and I believe that the body should be regarded morally as on loan from the biomass to the individual of whom it is, during life, a part. Previously a matter of only academic interest, this is now of immense practical importance. I have no problem with the right of the individual to bodily inviolability during life; integrity of the body is a necessary part of integrity of the person, together with the individual freedoms that are commonly stated in charters of rights and the like. I am deeply concerned with the right of the person to govern disposal of their body after death, when separation of body and soul is irrevocably complete, and the individual is incapable of reconstitution. The person no longer exists, the soul has departed, and the individual who was but is no longer has no further use for the body which has been part of him or her during life. The concept of the right of a person to determine before death, the disposal of their body after death, made sense only when there was no continuing use for that body; it makes neither practical nor moral sense now, when the body for which the dead person no longer has any use, is quite literally a vital resource, a potential source of life for others. Another way of looking at the cadaver, is to liken it to a dress or a suit of clothes hanging in a closet, worn by the person during life, evocative of pleasant experiences and happy times, but now no longer needed by the one who has died and useful only as a memorial by the bereaved. If it can help to keep the living warm, should not this be done? Is this not both practically and morally, its right utilisation?

"I regard the rights of the potential recipient, because of the benefits accruing, to be pre-emptive over all others."

If this argument is correct, then it is even more morally unacceptable for the relatives of the deceased to deny utilisation of the cadaver as a source of transplantable organs. Their only claim upon it is as a temporary memorial of a loved one, inevitably destined to decay or be burned in a very short time. To me, any such claim cannot morally be sustained in the face of what I regard as the overwhelming and pre-emptive need of the potential recipient. It is particularly unacceptable when the deceased has during life expressed consent for cadaver organ donation, and still unacceptable if he or she has expressed no opinion. The need of the potential recipient, the benefit which may accrue to him or her, to me trumps and surpasses all other considerations. The proportionate benefit is too great to be subordinate to anything else. This can be expressed in a simple parable. A rich man has a loaf which he does not need, which he cannot eat, for which he has no use. To a poor man, starving, the gift of this loaf would be the gift of life itself. But the rich man says: "I will not give you this loaf; I will drop it on the dunghill to decay, or fling it in the fire to burn". This is to me a specific analogy of the denial of organ donation, of the conscious refusal to grant it. In many instances the denial is not conscious, a positive act, but a negative omission, a failure to consider and decide upon the possibility before it becomes real. It is commonplace that there is a great gap between the proportion of people in a society who favour organ donation, and the much smaller proportion who do anything about it.

In my opinion the human cadaver, at the point at which life departs, should become a resource for those who may benefit from donation of its organs. Our society has conspicuously failed to achieve this by voluntary means, and the increasing length of the queues for donated organs testifies eloquently to this failure. On the other hand, a majority of the community express their belief that cadaver organs should be used for transplantation. Faced with this contradiction and the dilemma so caused, it appears to be morally and practically necessary for society to act to overcome this failure, and this could best be done by making the human cadaver the charge and responsibility of the state, to determine its best disposition. Without going into detail, it might be done by establishing an organisation for this purpose, under the authority of the state but at "arm's length", very strictly separated from government and politics.

Refusal Is Immoral

The rights and responsibilities of disposal of the cadaver should be vested in this organisation. When the cadaver has been used, if possible, as a source of transplantable organs it may, if the family wishes, be reconsigned to their care, for such religious and social observances as they desire. Practically, this might be welcomed by many, as removing the necessity for an agonising decision by the family. Also practically, it is impossible for the family, in such circumstances, to be able to tell what has been done; after routine autopsy the body is reconstituted so that there is no outward sign, to ordinary observation such as that at an open coffin funeral or memorial service, that any examination has been performed. Legally, this might be regarded as an extension of the doctrine of Parens patriae, the assumption by the state of parental responsibility when this is necessary, on behalf of the persons benefiting from organ donation and transplantation. Morally, I regard the rights of the potential recipient, because of the benefits accruing, to be pre-emptive over all others.

In this situation, the idea of consent and its corollary, refusal are not morally applicable. One may be able to give or refuse consent to a procedure which affects oneself, but organ donation affects no one physically; no human person is involved as donor. To grant the right and power of consent to an individual who may be affected emotionally, is to elevate the possible emotional affect of one person, as more important than the physical life of another. The imbalance of benefit is too great to permit of this, and I find it morally unacceptable. To require consent for cadaver organ donation from the one of whose person in life the body is a part, is unacceptably to extend control of that body beyond legitimate limits. To require consent from the relatives of a previously living person is unacceptably to extend their control over matters where the good of others should be the predominant concern. The concept of consent in this situation is morally incorrect.

This having been said, in a society which places predominant value in autonomy, it may not be possible to enact in law what is morally correct. Should this matter ever attain the status of a legislative proposal, as it has in some countries, it might be a practical necessity to extend the principle of autonomy to a right to refusal of cadaver organ donation, to a living individual—to legitimise, in effect, the attitude of the rich man in my parable. To me this would be immoral, but it might be necessary to condone this limited immorality, commonly expressed as the right to opt out, or to refuse, to the individual. It would be a limited sacrifice to the much greater good.

Removing Vital Organs from Living Donors Is Unethical

by John A. Robertson

About the author: *John A. Robertson is a professor at the University of Texas Law School and the author of* Children of Choice: Freedom and the New Reproductive Technologies.

Although living persons donate kidneys, cadaveric donors are the main source of solid organs for transplantation. Yet cadaveric donations have never been sufficient to meet the needs of persons with end-stage organ disease. One factor among many that limits the availability of cadaveric organs is the dead donor rule—the ethical and legal rule that requires that donors not be killed in order to obtain their organs.

Laws and norms against homicide forbid killings done for any purpose, including killings done to obtain organs to save the life of others. These laws and norms apply even if the person is unconscious, extremely debilitated, or very near death. The effect is to create the dead donor rule—the rule that states that organ retrieval itself cannot cause death. Removal of organs necessary for life prior to demise would violate the dead donor rule regardless of the condition or consent of the donor because removal of those organs would kill the donor. Removal of nonvital organs prior to death would not violate the rule, though it would implicate other laws and ethical norms.

Laws and norms against killing are most clearly applicable when the person killed has not consented to the killing. But they also apply when a person requests death, whether to avoid suffering or to provide organs for transplant. The dead donor rule would thus prevent a person from committing suicide in order to provide organs to his family or others. In the short run the rule is deontologic

John A. Robertson, "The Dead Donor Rule," *Hastings Center Report*, November 1999. Copyright © 1999 by the Hastings Center. Reproduced by permission.

rather than utilitarian, for it prevents the killing of one person for organs that would save the three or more lives that can be saved by a single cadaveric donor.

Central to Organ Donation Ethics

The dead donor rule is a center piece of the social order's commitment to respect for persons and human life. It is also the ethical linchpin of a voluntary system of organ donation, and helps maintain public trust in the organ procurement system. Although it is possible that some changes in the dead donor rule could be adopted without a major reduction in protection of persons and public trust, changes in the rule should be measured by their effect on both those functions.

Several recent proposals to increase the supply of cadaveric organs would create exceptions to the dead donor rule to allow donation when the donor lacks an upper brain and will imminently die (anencephalic infants) or will be executed (death row prisoners). These proposals do not challenge the rule's core function of protecting persons against unwanted demise. They do not, for example, propose a "survival lottery" in which persons are picked by chance to be killed to provide organs to several others. Nor would they permit competent persons to choose suicide by organ retrieval in order to save others. Instead, they would modify the rule at the margins of human life.

Proposals to permit donation from anencephalic infants or condemned prisoners aim to maintain respect for the core values underlying the dead donor rule while concluding that the benefits of relaxing the rule in these marginal cases outweigh the loss in respect for life and trust in the transplant system that might result. In contrast, proposals to retrieve organs from non-heart-beating donors claim to respect the dead donor rule as such by permitting organ retrieval only after the donor has been pronounced dead on cardiopulmonary grounds. Ethical controversy arises there, however, because uncertainties in determining cardiopulmonary death create a risk that the donor will not be dead when organ retrieval occurs, but will die as a result of the retrieval itself.

A closely related question concerns whether it is ethically acceptable for physicians to implement proposals that violate the dead donor rule in these marginal cases. From the time of Hippocrates, codes of medical ethics have condemned killing by physicians. This tradition continues strongly today in medical, ethical, and legal opposition to active euthanasia, physician-assisted suicide, and the participation of physicians in capital punishment and torture. If the dead donor rule is relaxed to facilitate organ procurement in these marginal cases, it will require a concomitant relaxation in prohibitions against physicians killing. Many persons would count such a change as an additional reason for opposing exceptions to the dead donor rule.

Incompetent Persons and the Dead Donor Rule

The dead donor rule limits only organ retrieval that causes death. It says nothing about situations in which organ retrieval itself would not cause death. Removing nonessential organs or tissue from incompetent persons on the basis of substituted consent—for example, retrieving kidneys from retarded individuals or from those in persistent vegetative states—would not violate the dead donor rule because organ or tissue retrieval in those cases would not cause death. Retrieval of nonessential organs would, however, implicate concerns about showing proper respect for the dignity and well-being of incompetent persons, for example, not treating them as mere means to the ends of others. Although it would not violate the dead donor rule, retrieval in such cases still could not occur unless applicable ethical and legal requirements for consent by the donor or family had been met.

Some persons have mistakenly viewed the dead donor rule as also prohibiting retrieval of nonessential organs from comatose or incompetent persons prior to their death because ordinarily such organs are removed only after death has occurred. The fact that organ and tissue retrieval usually occurs after death, however, does not mean that retrieval cannot occur before death if ethical and legal norms for what may be done to persons prior to their death are observed.

An example that nicely illustrates the distinction between the dead donor rule and rules for respecting incompetent persons would arise in a situation in which a family member, say the father, would like to donate a kidney to his daughter who suffers from end-stage kidney disease and who is not tolerating dialysis well. Medical examination shows that he has a serious heart condition that rules him out as a live donor. Soon after, he suffers a massive cardiac arrest that leaves him in a permanent coma in which he can be maintained indefinitely.

"The dead donor rule is . . . the ethical linchpin of a voluntary system of organ donation."

At this point, removal of a kidney from him for transplantation to his daughter would not violate the dead donor rule because it would not cause his death. Whether it is ethically and legally acceptable, however, would depend on whether removal is consistent with laws and norms for respecting the interests of incompetent persons. In this case, based on his prior expressed wishes to donate to his daughter and the absence of harm to him from the donation, a plausible claim can be made that removal of the kidney is ethically and legally acceptable. If this option were not acceptable to the family, they could request that he be treated as a non-heart-beating donor, that is, have life support stopped, and then retrieve his kidney after he has been pronounced dead.

A key factor in observing the dead donor rule is the determination of death. The United States and most European countries now accept that death can be determined by tests that show irreversible cessation of circulatory and respiratory function or irreversible cessation of all functions of the entire brain. The latter tests—tests for whole-brain death—are necessary when the irreversible cessation of cardiopulmonary functions in a mechanically assisted patient cannot be independently established. . . .

Anencephalic Infants

One proposal to change the dead donor rule would allow the retrieval of vital organs from anencephalic infants before they have suffered whole-brain death. Because few children die in circumstances where brain death is pronounced, organs for pediatric transplant, where organ size is a crucial factor, are in very short supply. Faced with the shortage of pediatric hearts, one center tried unsuccessfully to transplant a heart from a baboon to an infant with hypoplastic heart disease. Because of medical and ethical opposition to further use of xenografts, the center then proposed with parental consent to use organs from anencephalic newborns who had expired after treatment was withdrawn. When it was found that viable organs could not be obtained from anencephalic infants after death, consideration turned to removing organs before brain stem activity had ceased.

> *"A key factor in observing the dead donor rule is the determination of death."*

Such an alternative, however, is blocked by the dead donor rule. Although anencephalics lack an upper brain, they do have brain stem function, and thus are legally alive under existing criteria and tests for whole-brain death. Removing hearts and livers from anencephalic infants prior to total brain death would thus violate the dead donor rule and could be punishable as homicide. If anencephalics were to be a viable source of organs for pediatric transplant, an exception to the dead donor rule would have to be enacted into law and incorporated into ethical norms. . . .

Strong arguments . . . exist against recognizing an exception. A primary one is the need to keep a bright line against killing individuals who are alive. Opponents also cite the difficulties in diagnosing anencephaly and the corresponding risk of mistaken diagnoses, the small number of children who would benefit, and the risk that this exception would make it much more likely that additional exceptions to the dead donor rule would be enacted for those in persistent vegetative states or with severe, irreversible mental illnesses. An exception might also reinforce public fears that the interests of organ donors would be sacrificed to obtain organs, and violate symbolic concerns for showing respect for human life by not killing. Finally, physicians would, in the very act of retrieving vital organs, be killing the anencephalic patient.

The arguments against recognizing an exception to the dead donor rule for anencephalic infants have carried the day. For example, the favorable 1992 opinion of the Council on Ethical and Judicial Affairs of the American Medical Association was withdrawn in the face of wide opposition and never reissued. . . .

An additional factor conserving the dead donor rule in the case of anencephalic infants is the necessity for the government openly to authorize a change in the definition of death or in the law of homicide to allow killing by organ retrieval of anencephalic infants. Even if legal immunity from prosecution were provided, medical opposition to physicians removing organs that cause an anencephalic child's death might still continue. Indeed, transplant physicians might refuse to retrieve or use organs from anencephalics to prevent erosion of public trust in the organ donation and transplant system. . . .

Retrieving Organs from Executed Inmates

With over 3,200 persons now awaiting execution in the United States and some forty to seventy-five prisoners executed each year, proposals to retrieve organs for transplant from capital punishment have surfaced in recent years. The idea gained slight momentum in the early 1990s when a condemned prisoner in Georgia offered to donate organs as part of his execution and sued unsuccessfully for the opportunity. Bills to permit organ retrievals from executions have been introduced in a few state legislatures.

In considering proposals to use the organs of condemned prisoners, we must distinguish procuring organs from executed prisoners after their death or during their lives from procuring organs from them as a form of execution. There is no ethical or legal objection to removing organs or tissue from executed bodies after death, if consent of the deceased or next of kin has been obtained. Although most methods of execution would render organs unacceptable for transplant, the unclaimed bodies of executed inmates are routinely given to medical schools for anatomical study. Nor is there any ethical bar to a condemned prisoner serving as a living donor of a kidney or tissue, as long as the prisoner freely consents. Indeed, Texas and other capital punishment states permit live donations from condemned prisoners.

The question of execution by organ retrieval is quite different. To avoid the damaging effects on organs from execution by lethal injection, electrocution, hanging, gas, or firing squad, organ retrieval itself would become the method of execution. The condemned prisoner would request this method five to seven days before the execution date. At the time selected for execution, the prisoner would be taken from death row to the prison hospital and strapped on a gurney as in preparation for execution by lethal injection. Witnesses to the execution, including the victim's family, could view the insertion of intravenous lines and administration of anesthetic outside of the operating room. When the prisoner became unconscious, he would be moved to an operating room where the transplant team would then remove all his organs. When organ removal was completed, ventilatory or other mechanical assistance would be terminated, as occurs in retrieval from brain-dead, heart-beating cadavers. Death would be pronounced as having occurred either at the time that the heart and lungs were removed, or when mechanical assistance was terminated. The retrieved organs would then be distributed to consenting recipients

> *"Removing hearts and livers from anencephalic infants prior to total brain death would . . . violate the dead donor rule."*

in accordance with existing rules for distributing organs.

Such a procedure would clearly violate the dead donor rule. Retrieval of vital organs itself would be the cause of death because once heart, lungs, and liver are removed one would soon have to turn off the heart-lung bypass machines that are sustaining function during removal of vital organs. Physicians retrieving organs would thus also be executing the prisoner. For such a procedure to be acceptable, an exception to the dead donor rule in the case of executions would have to be recognized.

Opposition to Execution by Organ Retrieval

The main argument for an exception in this case is that the prisoner will in any case be executed. An exception to the rule to permit a mode of execution that protects organs would not harm the prisoner or deprive him of continued life, and thus would not infringe or deny the core values underlying the dead donor rule. The state in any case will be executing the prisoner, and the exception would permit the state to kill another in a way that salvages his organs. In addition, an exception for execution by organ retrieval has the salutary effect of respecting and preserving the lives of recipients at the very moment that the condemned person's life is taken as punishment for his having previously taken the life of others. . . .

The opponents of execution by organ retrieval have prevailed, and are likely to prevail for some time to come. The great aversion to an exception to the dead donor rule in the case of lawful executions is not adequately explained by the values underlying the dead donor rule. If state employees may legally kill a condemned criminal by drug, gas, or more violent means, it should not matter that execution occurs by removal of vital organs. This would not constitute an unconstitutional "cruel or unusual" punishment because there is nothing crueler about this method of execution, chosen by the prisoner, than other methods.

A stronger ground for opposition is the role that transplant physicians and nurses would necessarily play in a system of execution by organ retrieval. Execution by organ retrieval could not be carried out by non-physician executioners as now occurs with execution by lethal injection and other methods. Even if some transplant doctors and nurses who accept the moral validity of capital punishment might be willing to participate in organ retrieval executions, their participation would violate medical ethical pronouncements against the participation of physicians in executions. The execution would also have to occur in the operating room of a hospital. If the prison hospital lacked adequate facilities, a hospital willing to allow organ retrieval executions on its premises would have to be found—and it is likely that few transplant teams or hospitals would be willing to participate.

Opposition to such an exception also arises from the need to keep the death penalty separate from other social institutions. The death penalty is highly problematic morally, legally, and socially in those states that allow it; it would

97

become even more so if it also served as a method of organ procurement. Interjecting transplantation into the controversy over capital punishment could also taint public perceptions of the beneficence of transplantation. Members of the public might come to view organ procurement teams as "killers" who harvest organs before or after death. Such a perception could reduce the willingness of families to donate, and thus impair the prospects of persons awaiting transplants. The purpose and effect of capital punishment is to end the life of a person who has himself taken life. Trying at the same time to preserve other lives through execution by organ retrieval only confuses the situation. It is best for organ transplantation and capital punishment to go their separate ways.

Non-Heart-Beating Donors

Another proposal to increase the supply of cadaveric organs for transplant focusing attention on the dead donor rule is the use of non-heart-beating cadavers as organ donors. The first cadaveric organ donors were persons declared dead on cardiopulmonary criteria, who either suffered cardiac arrest in the hospital or who arrived there dead. With the acceptance of whole-brain criteria of death, organ procurement shifted to heart-beating cadaveric donors—those persons who were found to be brain-dead while cardiopulmonary functions were mechanically sustained. The shortage of brain-dead heart-beating donors has now refocused attention on the use of non-heart-beating donors (NHBDs).

The use of NHBDs that implicates the dead donor rule involves those cases that are planned or controlled, as opposed to those persons who are brought to the hospital dead. These protocols developed out of family requests to donate organs in situations in which it was unlikely that death would be pronounced on brain death grounds, thus preventing solid organ donation from occurring. Organ donation is a significant positive experience for those facing the death of a loved one; if these families are to have that positive experience, organ donation would have to occur immediately after death has been declared subsequent to withdrawal of life support—the non-heart-beating donor situation.

> *"It is best for organ transplantation and capital punishment to go their separate ways."*

In controlled NHBD cases a family requests that treatment be withdrawn from a loved one who is terminally ill but not brain dead and that his or her organs then be donated for transplant. To minimize warm ischemic time damaging to organs, ventilatory assistance to the patient may be withdrawn in the operating room, where the family may choose to be present. After withdrawal of life support, the patient's attending physician, who is not part of the organ recovery team, determines whether the heart and respiration have stopped. The physician will then pronounce the patient dead or, to provide an additional margin of safety, in some cases will wait an additional two to five minutes after cardiac function has stopped before pronouncing death. At this point the physician and any family that is present would withdraw, and the transplant team, which has been prepped and waiting in an adjoining room, will enter and retrieve organs from the recently dead cadaver. Studies have shown that organs retrieved in this way suffer little damage and are viable for transplant. . . .

The Controversy Over NHBDs

Ethical and legal controversy surrounds the use of controlled NHBDs because of the fear that retrieval of organs in the controlled setting could violate the dead donor rule, in either of two ways. One was that the drugs administered prior to death in NHBD protocols—anticoagulants (heparin) and vasodilators (regitine) to minimize the effects of warm ischemia on organ viability—could hasten or even cause death. . . .

Transplant physicians with experience with these drugs deny that they are administered to hasten death or that they are given in such doses that they could have that effect, and the IOM [Institute of Medicine] found that administering heparin and regitine prior to death to preserve organs generally does not harm the donor and is justifiable as part of routine preparation for organ retrieval. . . . Careful attention to whether such drugs need to be administered to the near-death patient to preserve organs and whether the dosages used are contraindicated because of the patient's condition should minimize the risk that efforts to preserve organs prior to death will inadvertently violate the dead donor rule.

A second way in which NHBD protocols are said to violate the dead donor rule is that they allow retrieval of organs before cessation of pulmonary function is irreversible. The risk is that death will be pronounced so quickly after the removal of life support and induction of cardiac arrest that the person will not have irreversibly lost cardiac function and thus will still be alive when organs are removed. That is, the person will appear to be dead, but might actually, if given longer time to breathe on his own or if immediately resuscitated, regain spontaneous respiration and circulation. If organ retrieval has already begun in such patients, retrieval will then be the cause of death, thus violating the dead donor rule.

To guard against such mistakes, NHBD programs have traditionally waited a few minutes after determining that cardiopulmonary function has ceased before pronouncing death and beginning organ retrieval. . . .

The debate over the use of NHBDs shows that their use in accordance with guidelines such as those recommended by the IOM does comply with the dead donor rule. Unlike the case of anencephaly, where the donor is clearly alive under whole-brain criteria of death when vital organs are taken, the use of NHBDs involves: no violation of the dead donor rule and requires no public alteration or exception to it. Nevertheless, it is important that NHBDs are used only according to publicly announced protocols that contain clear procedures for minimizing the risk of any such violations. Such protocols should require that death is pronounced according to the attending physician's judgment without pressure from transplant personnel, that tests and waiting periods are used that are reasonably certain to correctly ascertain cardiopulmonary death, and that administration of anticoagulants or vasodilators does not occur in circumstances that might hasten death or harm patients.

The Future of the Dead Donor Rule

The dead donor rule plays an important role in protecting persons and engendering trust in a voluntary system of organ donation. Any change in the rule to increase organ supply requires convincing evidence that more benefit than harm to persons and the transplant system would result from such a change. Even then, strong resistance to modifying the rule would exist based on the prudential and symbolic advantages of strict maintenance of a rule against death by organ retrieval.

It is thus no surprise that none of the proposals for explicit exceptions to the dead donor rule have been adopted. Removing vital organs from anencephalic infants requires public recognition that such lives are so diminished or lacking in value that they may be killed for their organs. Although these newborns will imminently die and will suffer no harm from retrieval of vital organs, the symbolic costs of relaxing the dead donor rule appear to be too great to be tolerated. Similarly, organ retrieval executions have little support, despite their attempt to wring some good from society's deliberate taking of life.

> *"The conservative posture that now exists toward maintaining the dead donor rule is likely to continue for some time, but not because of logical necessity."*

The use of NHBDs, on the other hand, is morally and legally acceptable because of their careful attempt to respect the dead donor rule. The debate over the use of NHBDs, however, illustrates the strong opposition that probably would exist if vital organs were taken from non-heart-beating donors who were not dead or if drugs administered to preserve organs also caused death. Despite the briefness and poor quality of the life remaining to such donors, violation of the dead donor rule would most likely be as strongly opposed here as it is with anencephalic infants.

The conservative posture that now exists toward maintaining the dead donor rule is likely to continue for some time, but not because of logical necessity. One could imagine that the question of how strictly the dead donor rule should be adhered to in order to maintain respect for persons and trust in the organ procurement system might be answered differently as medical, ethical, and social conditions and perceptions change. We might, for example, come to accept that persons who have only brain stem function or who are permanently unconscious are so close to being dead that we are willing to take their vital organs when clear benefits to others could be shown. Opponents or proponents of capital punishment might come to accept the need to save lives even as executions occur, and support execution by organ retrieval. Only a slight shift in attitude would then be needed to view the transplant team's role in executions as life-affirming, just as it is in organ retrievals from brain-dead, heart-beating cadavers whose cardiopulmonary functions are ended by organ retrieval. Such shifts in the strictness of the dead donor rule could occur without impairing respect for human life generally or diluting perceptions of physicians as healers, because the life at stake in these cases is so marginal in quality or expectancy and the resulting preservation of life in recipients is so significant.

Yet it is highly unlikely that such changes in perception or practice will soon occur. The symbolic importance of the dead donor rule is so great that even the slightest explicit deviation from it confronts a very high presumption of unacceptability. An important factor in strictly maintaining the rule is the small number of lives that would be saved as a result. With roughly fifty executions and fifty anencephalic births occurring each year, and only a portion of these prisoners or families likely to opt for organ donation, relatively few lives would be saved at the price of crossing an important symbolic threshold. Of course, any additional contribution to the pool of donor organs is welcome. Each cadaveric donor made possible by changes in the dead donor rule could save or extend the lives of three or more existing individuals. But saving the lives of others, as the dead donor rule itself shows, has never been a uniformly privileged activity. Efforts to increase organ supply would be more fruitfully directed to increasing acceptance of NHBDs and the desirability of donating organs generally than to changing the dead donor rule.

Chapter 3

Are Reproductive Technologies Ethical?

Chapter Preface

Genetic engineering has been a topic of interest and concern among the scientific and medical community for nearly four decades. However, it has only been within the last several years, with the mapping of the human genome, that society has been able to consider the real possibility of creating children with specific characteristics. It is now possible for parents undergoing in vitro fertilization to select embryos of a particular sex prior to implantation. As reproductive technology evolves, parents may one day be able to design their offspring, choosing traits ranging from preferred hair color, to high intelligence, to artistic ability. The benefits of such genetic engineering are questioned by many ethicists, however, who raise concerns about the effects reproductive technology will have on society.

Arguments in favor of genetic engineering center on the idea of improving humans. For example, many supporters point out that genetic engineering can prevent the births of infants afflicted with Tay-Sachs or other fatal or debilitating diseases. Another argument, whose advocates include Nobel Prize winner James Watson, is that if humans can find a way to improve the species, then it is immoral not to do so. Watson contends, "[It is] true moral cowardice to allow children to be born with known genetic defects."

Critics of advanced reproductive technologies, however, are concerned that genetic engineering would ultimately corrupt and divide society. Bioethicist Gilbert Meilaender, in an essay published in the religious magazine *First Things*, asserts that the ability of parents to design only the children they want, and to reject or abort those that do not meet their requirements, has distorted both childhood and parenthood. He writes, "The unconditional character of maternal and paternal love is replaced by choice, quality control, and an only conditional acceptance." Caroline S. Wagner, a Europe-based researcher, observes in an article in the *Los Angeles Times* that genetic alteration will create social imbalances. According to Wagner, only wealthy families will be able to afford such procedures. As a result, she asserts, "They will use technology to ensure that their children have significantly more advantages than the random mix of the gene pool, widening the gap between rich and poor. What then becomes of the notion that we are all created equal?"

Human gene manipulation is at least a decade or two away, so for now most of the arguments both for and against it are hypothetical. However, prospective parents have shown a willingness to embrace such procedures, as their use of existing reproductive technologies illustrates, and thus the ethical issues surrounding advancements in reproduction cannot be ignored. In the following chapter the authors debate whether reproductive technologies are moral or if they run counter to the appropriate goals of medicine.

Fear of Reproductive Technologies Is Unfounded

by Robin Marantz Henig

About the author: *Robin Marantz Henig is a science writer.*

The world's first test tube baby turns 25 this week [in July 2003]. You might know her name—Louise Brown—and that the pair of doctors responsible for her birth sounded vaguely like an old vaudeville team. You might know that those doctors, Steptoe and Edwards, were from Britain; if you were alive at the time, you might even remember that the city where they did their experiments, and where Louise was born, was Oldham.

But what you probably don't know, or don't remember, is how frightening it was to wait for that landmark birth. Most of those who were paying attention, from scientists to church officials to editorial writers, were sure that the world's first test tube baby would be abnormal; genetically deformed, less-than-human, monstrous, at the very least a freak of nature who would have to grow up with the eyes of the world charting its every move.

Amazingly, Louise was pink and perfect, normal in every way. When she arrived just before midnight on July 25, 1978, with 10 fingers, 10 toes and a lovely, lusty cry, she was graphic evidence that lab manipulations didn't have to harm the embryo. The age of assisted reproduction had begun.

Similar Fears

The fears that preceded Louise's birth are similar to the fears today about other reproductive technologies. Some of the voices currently raised in opposition to the thorniest interventions—cloning and designer babies in particular—are the very same voices raised a generation ago in opposition to in vitro fertilization (IVF). And some of these voices are saying the very same things now that they were saying in the 1970s. But even if the players and the rhetoric are the same, the situation is not. We are, it seems, on the verge of learning the wrong lessons from the IVF experience, bending too far in the direction of over-regulating reproductive research because we have seen the unfortunate results of underregulation.

Listen, for example, to Leon Kass, a bioethics professor at the University of Chicago whose voice has been part of this debate for 25 years. "More is at stake [with IVF research] than in ordinary biomedical research or in experimenting with human subjects at risk of bodily harm," Kass testified before the federal government's Ethics Advisory Board shortly after Louise Brown's birth. "At stake is the idea of the humanness of our human life and the meaning of our embodiment, our sexual being, and our relation to ancestors and descendants."

The Slippery Slope Argument

Kass is now President [George W.] Bush's leading bioethics advisor, and when he talks about cloning he uses many of the same words he used in 1978. He sees moral ruin and calamity in the petri dishes where human embryos grow. Now as then, his concerns can be expressed in a simple shorthand: He worries about the so-called slippery slope.

The term implies a certain inevitability to scientific progress, an inability to put a stop to increasingly more loathsome applications of knowledge once we achieve that knowledge. If the slope of progress is indeed slippery, then any first step—even if it is not objectionable when considered in isolation—becomes objectionable because it could lead to some sort of abuse.

The slippery slope argument emerges often in scientific history, whenever a powerful new development might have dreadful ramifications. People talked about the slippery slope since the first artificial insemination was publicized in 1909, conjuring images of selective breeding and a race of illegitimate souls. They talked about it after the first heart transplant in 1967, after the first animal-to-human transplant in 1984, and, in 2002, after the first transplanted uterus. Early cases of assisted suicide stimulated talk about a slippery slope that would lead to wholesale killing of the aged or infirm; early attempts at amniocentesis begat fears about a slippery slope toward the elimination of fetuses that were imperfect in some way—or that were simply the "wrong" sex.

> *"Fear of . . . horrors should not cause us to prohibit procedures that are in themselves innocuous."*

To be sure, some of these first steps have led to brutal applications—abortions of female fetuses in China and India, for example, and shameful experiences with eugenics around the world—but fear of such horrors should not cause us to prohibit procedures that are in themselves innocuous, and that might easily lead to enhancement of our collective fate rather than to devastation.

If IVF was the first step down a slippery slope of its own, then it seems to have landed us in exactly the spot that Kass and others said it would. Earlier [in

July 2003] this month two reports from the annual meeting of the European Society of Human Reproduction and Embryology made it seem that fun-with-embryos had gotten a little out of hand. An American scientist, Norbert Gleicher, announced that he and his colleagues had successfully inserted cells from a male embryo into an early-stage female embryo, creating a mixed-gender chimera that some journalists called a "she-male." Another team, from Israel and the Netherlands, described a trick that was even more bizarre: harvesting eggs from aborted fetuses and culturing them so they could be used in IVF, thereby creating a baby with a biological mother who had never been born.

No one would be talking about "she-male" embryos or fetal mothers if the techniques of IVF hadn't been perfected over the past quarter-century. These newer maneuvers, as well as all the others that most frighten people, begin with the same steps used for IVF: extraction of the eggs and sperm, fertilization in a petri dish, culture of the embryo until it reaches a certain stage and, finally, implantation into a receptive uterus. Of the scenarios that are now causing so much anxiety—cloning, pre-implantation genetic diagnosis, genetic engineering of sex cells, the creation of human/animal hybrids, the culturing of human embryos as a source of replacement parts—none is possible without the techniques of basic IVF: laboratory fertilization and embryo transfer.

IVF Without Standards

Even if a slippery slope exists, it cannot be allowed to dictate science policy. Regulating something that can be done now on the basis of fears about what might be done later is a mistake. And it can result in some unintended and paradoxical effects. For all the railing against IVF in the '70s, the protests led to less control over IVF rather than more. Early on, opponents thought the best way to stop troublesome science was to keep the federal government from financing it, and they fought against using taxpayer money for research involving fetuses or embryos—which, by extension, included IVF. One by one, a succession of bioethics commissions were formed to review these bans; one by one, the commissions recommended that the bans be lifted.

But politicians, some of whom were afraid of alienating a vocal anti-abortion lobby opposed to the experimental use of fetuses and embryos, generally did not want to hear that they should underwrite such controversial research. As a result, a pattern developed for the bioethicists' role in the regulatory minuet: sit on a commission, hold meetings, attend public hearings, write a report that says the research is ethically acceptable, have the report ignored, watch the next president or Congress convene a new commission, and repeat.

Even after the fetal research ban was lifted, and then the embryo research ban, the government still refused to sponsor IVF research. But the lack of federal support for IVF didn't stop scientists from working on it—it just led them to carry on beneath the radar, out of the reach of the main mechanism for oversight, which was (and still is) the federal research grant and the standards it imposes on its recipients. If no one was getting government grants for IVF, then no one was being required to adhere to any standards. Entrepreneurial scientists were doing IVF anyway, bolstered by private money from infertile couples desperate for babies. Most of these scientists were honorable men and women with solid reputations and the loftiest of goals. A few, however, were motivated by the things that drive so many innovators, scientists included—ego, curiosity, ambition, even greed. They were free agents who essentially did whatever they wanted and whatever the market would bear. Their efforts turned some of the fertility industry into a cowboy science driven by supply and demand. . . .

Miraculous Treatments

As the world's first test tube baby turns 25, half a million others born through assisted reproductive technology can raise a glass in celebration of the new treatments for infertility that have subsequently developed. The agony of childlessness, for a couple that wants children, has been greatly eased because of the path blazed by Louise Brown's doctors, and her parents, too, who didn't even realize at first that they were involved in an enterprise that had never worked before. And look at all that has followed. Much of it might have been troublesome, but much more of it has been miraculous.

Happy birthday, Louise.

Sex Selection Is Ethical

by George Dvorsky

About the author: *George Dvorsky is the deputy editor of Betterhumans, an editorial production company that provides information and analysis on the effects of science and technology.*

Several years ago, good friends of mine were desperate to conceive a girl. To improve the odds, they tried what is known as the Shettles Method.

The Shettles Method

This method, developed by Landrum Shettles, suggests that the timing and position of intercourse can help couples determine a baby's gender.

Shettles notes that the X-bearing (female) sperm are hardier and slower moving than the Y-bearing (male) sperm. Accordingly, he proposes that couples who want a girl should have sex two or more days before ovulation. The reasoning is that when the egg finally arrives, there's an increased chance that only the female sperm will be around to fertilize it.

Additionally, because X sperm are more resilient than Y sperm, Shettles recommends that couples use the missionary position to keep sperm further away from the cervix. He also suggests that women avoid having an orgasm, as it increases the alkaline secretions that tend to favour Y sperm. (Sorry ladies.)

Couples the world-over have tried the Shettles Method and countless other techniques to exert at least some control over the sex of their offspring. And for as long as women have been making babies, they have been exchanging ideas about how to conceive a boy or a girl.

Shettles claims that his technique tips the odds of any one gender from 50% to 75%. Using the technique, my friends did in fact conceive a girl, and were absolutely delighted. Many experts dismiss the practice, however, claiming that it does nothing to improve the odds.

More sophisticated technologies available at fertility clinics, such as the Albumin or MicroSort sperm separation methods, undoubtedly do. Clinical gender selection finally offers couples the chance to definitively decide the gender of their offspring without having to rely on untrustworthy techniques.

Stubborn and Ignorant Responses

But despite the fact that they build on a long tradition and that a strong demand exists for them, gender selection technologies may be illegal if you live in a country such as Canada. Thanks to Health Minister Anne McLellan and the federal Liberal party, Canada is on the verge of seeing Bill C-13—the so-called "Assisted Human Reproduction Act"—voted into law, effectively criminalizing clinical gender selection.[1]

Yes, that's correct: Offering couples a proven means of choosing the sex of their children is soon to become a codified criminal offense in Canada, while unproven means will remain legal.

It's unbelievable. Gender selection is perhaps the most straightforward and harmless assistive reproductive procedure around. Should Bill C-13 be voted into law, it would represent a significant setback in the struggle to see germinal choice technologies receive social and political sanction.

Moreover, attempts to criminalize this and other viable reproductive options expose the irrational stubbornness and rampant ignorance that is so characteristic of biofundamentalism in both Canada and the United States. If our politicians can't get their heads around something as elementary and clear-cut as the right to choose the gender of offspring, what does it say about the potential for more significant germinal choice technologies and human re-engineering?

Absurd Arguments

There are virtually no good arguments for opposing gender selection, making the current resistance to it all the more unfathomable.

James Grifo, president-elect of the Society for Assisted Reproductive Technology and a reproductive endocrinologist, argues that "sex selection is sex discrimination," and has labeled it an unethical practice. "It's not ethical to take someone off the street and help them have a boy or a girl," says Grifo.

Like Grifo, many people are concerned that sex selection will result in possible sex ratio imbalances in the future, such as the ones that currently exist in China and India.

Others believe that gender selection imposes psychological harm to the sex-selected offspring by imposing unrealistic expectations upon them.

And yet others warn of increased marital conflict over gender selection decisions and a strengthening of gender bias in society as a whole.

"What's the next step?" asks William Schoolcraft of the Colorado Center for Reproductive Medicine in Englewood, and a supporter of Grifo. "As we learn more about genetics," asks Schoolcraft, "do we reject kids who do not have su-

---

1. The bill passed on October 28, 2003.

perior intelligence or who don't have the right color hair or eyes?"

Opponents of sex selection are essentially singing the tired old tune of slippery slopeism. They basically argue that once parents start choosing the characteristics of their offspring, discrimination against those who aren't "perfect" will soon follow.

How this catastrophic breakdown of civil rights is supposed to happen in our progressively cosmopolitan and tolerant liberal democracies is never elucidated. I simply don't buy the argument that increased reproductive options will cause society to regress back into 19th century mentalities.

Do Not Worry About Ratios

As for the argument about sex ratio imbalances, I'm not particularly worried. First, most couples in the West—those countries that tend to have tolerant people with enlightened perspectives on gender and race—simply want sex selection for what is known as "family balancing." Many couples simply want two kids: A boy and a girl.

> *"There are virtually no good arguments for opposing gender selection, making the current resistance to it all the more unfathomable."*

My grandmother produced four girls before she delivered a baby boy for my hopeful grandfather. While I love my aunts dearly, the keep-having-babies-until-you-get-the-one-you-want method seems rather excessive and unnecessary.

Also, the number of couples who choose to use clinical gender selection may turn out to be insignificant in reference to the six billion occupants of Earth. It simply won't result in any statistically significant change to the global sex ratio.

In the odd chance that sex selection does have an impact on gender ratios, the government could always step in and offer tax breaks to couples who choose to have children of the less-present gender.

And finally, the argument that premeditated characteristics cause parents to impose lofty expectations on their children is nonsense. Since time immemorial parents have imposed their own expectations upon their children. (Not to mention those stories of mothers dressing their little boys in dresses.) This would appear to be an issue of parenting skills and not reproductive rights.

Society Will Not Collapse

Simply put, gender selection causes no harm to anyone. And in fact, it may produce the opposite effect. Take my friends who wanted a baby girl, for example; while they would have welcomed a boy with open arms, once their expectations and hopes had been established, a second boy for them would have been a mixed blessing.

Opponents of sex selection don't have a foot to stand on, and this bodes well for the advent of germinal choice technologies.

Many arguments used against sex selection are used against genetic engineering, human cloning and other pending reproductive innovations.

Yes, some people want to choose the gender of their offspring. Yes, some people are going to want to choose the physical and cognitive characteristics of their children.

And no, contrary to hysterical belief, once these procedures are perfected, they will not harm children; no, society will not breakdown as the next generation of humans become healthier, stronger, smarter and happier.

Nor will society collapse as we progressively endow parents with greater biological autonomy and reproductive control.

A Threat to Bodily Sovereignty

In 1967, Canadian Prime Minister Pierre Trudeau famously said that "there is no place for the state in the bedrooms of the nation." While Trudeau was speaking about legalizing homosexuality, the spirit of his statement has been broadened by many Canadians to include not just sexual freedoms, but reproductive freedoms as well.

Unfortunately, Trudeau's Liberal party descendants have chosen to ignore his words and dismiss the brave path that he began forging over 30 years ago. Instead, Anne McLellan and the Liberals want to join Canadian couples in their bedrooms and snuggle up right between them. And this for no good reason, aside from the government's misguided patriarchal proclivities.

Here in Canada we are witnessing the Feds slip Bill C-13 by a largely unaware Canadian public. And by virtue of this ambivalence, Canadian couples are in effect opening the bedroom doors for the government to come right in.

But of course, we don't have to tolerate this. That's why elections were invented.

People of all nations should be wary of any attempt by their government to intervene and control their reproductive privileges and bodily sovereignty.

Gender selection is under attack, and citizens in democratic countries must fight back with government selection. If they restrict your reproductive rights, send them packing.

Human Reproductive Cloning Is Ethical

by Rael

About the author: *Rael is the head of the Raelian cult. The cult has claimed to have successfully cloned a human, although no definitive proof has been provided.*

Editor's Note: This viewpoint was originally given as testimony before the U.S. House of Representatives on March 28, 2001.

The conservative, orthodox, fanatic traditional religions have always tried to keep humanity in a primitive stage of darkness. It is easy to see that in countries like Afghanistan which are back to the middle ages due to a fanatic Moslem government.

Religion Is the Enemy of Science

But this was also true in occidental powers. The first medical doctors who tried to study the human by opening cadavers were excommunicated by the Catholic Church. It was considered a sin to try to unveil the mystery of the creation of god. . . . So were the first antibiotics, blood transfusions, vaccines, surgeries, contraception, organ transplants . . . religious fanatics were always saying that "it's a sin to go against the will of god. . . . If somebody is sick, let him die, his life is in god's hands."

If our civilization would have respected these primitive ideas from dark ages, we would all die around 35, and 9 out of 10 babies born would die in their first 2 years.

Traditional religions have always been against scientific progress. They were against the steam engine, electricity, airplanes, cars, radio, television, etc. . . . If we had listened to them we would still have horses and carts and candles. . . .

Twenty-two years ago they were against IVF [in vitro fertilization], talking about monsters, Frankenstein and playing god, and now IVF is well accepted,

Rael, testimony before the U.S. House of Representatives, Washington, DC, March 28, 2001.

performed every day by thousands and helping happy families with fertility problems to have babies.

Today human cloning will help other families to have children, and again they are against it. It will also help to cure numerous diseases, will help us live a lot longer, and finally will help us reach, in the future, eternal life.

Nothing should stop science, which should be 100 percent free.

Ethical Committees Are Harmful

Ethical committees are unnecessary and dangerous as they give power to conservative, obscurantist forces, which are guided only by traditional religious powers.

As well as there should be a complete separation of state and religion, there should also be a complete separation of science and state, or science and religion.

If there was an ethical committee when antibiotics, blood transfusions and vaccines were discovered it would have certainly been possible that these technologies would have been forbidden. You can imagine the poor health the world would be in today. . . .

Ethical committees should be necessary when a deadly technology is making the production of weapons of mass destruction possible. . . . And to my knowledge there are no ethical committees concerning nuclear, chemical or biological weapons. These things are created to kill millions of people and possibly destroy all life on earth. Cloning is a pro-life technology, a technology made to give birth to babies!

Cloning Benefits Families

The first benefit of human cloning is to make it possible for couples who cannot have children using other existing techniques to have babies inheriting genetic traits from one of their parents. They can be infertile heterosexual couples or gay couples.

The second benefit is for families who lose a child due to crime, accident or disease to have the same child brought back to life.

All conservative "pro-life" groups always talk about "the right of the unborn," but in this case we must talk about protecting the rights of the "unreborn." As cloning technology makes this possible, why should we accept the accidental death of a beloved child, when we can bring this very child back to life?

People who are opposed to it are always influenced by a terrible Judeo-Christian education . . . the same as those who could have made antibiotics, vaccines, transfusions, surgery and organ transplants forbidden. Their main objections are:

1. "It is an unsafe technology, which is not advanced enough": the best way to develop this technology like all other technologies is by doing it. The first surgeries, organ transplants, and IVF were unsuccessful. But by doing it, scientists were able to develop their expertise.

2. "It will create monsters": a percentage of "normally" (sexually) conceived babies are born "monsters" or with genetic faults. . . . Would you make a law against making babies sexually through the "natural" way because of these problems? Of course not and the percentage amongst cloned babies will be lower as they will be more precisely scrutinized from the first days after conception.

3. "The children made by cloning will have a terrible life being looked at as abnormal people": not more than IVF conceived children, or twins, or physically handicapped children or gay or colored people. It is not the problem of the children themselves, but the responsibility of the society to educate the public to respect the differences, all the differences, between human beings.

4. "It is against biodiversity to create cloned children, creating identical people": we have already on earth millions of twins and this is not a problem. The conception through cloning will always be used by a limited number of people and that will not affect biodiversity. But even if you imagine 6 billion human beings being cloned, the biodiversity is still the same as we still would be 6 billion different people!

5. "Cloned children will not be exactly the same": so what is the problem? As long as the families are informed about this, (and they are) there is absolutely no problem with that. People against cloning keep saying "it is terrible they will be the same" and then suddenly they argue "they will not be exactly the same." . . . So what is the problem?

6. "Cloned children will have terrible psychological problems being created to replace dead babies, but they will never be exactly the same": loving families who lose a child and want to have him back through cloning have so much love for this child, a child they hope so much to have back, that I cannot imagine a child being loved more. More than other families, those who lose a child due to disease or accident or crime have learned so much about how life is fragile, that they will protect and care for these children much more than "normal" families. And a good education is to accept that your children are not exactly what you would want them to be. "Normal" families experience that every day when a father who is a medical doctor sees his child only interested by music or painting, as the father was dreaming to have his son become a doctor like he is. . . . Real love is accepting the differences, and that includes the differences between the image you have of your child and who he really is.

> *"Cloning is a pro-life technology, a technology made to give birth to babies!"*

7. "Human cloning is unnatural": we already answered to this objection. Nor are blood transfusions, antibiotics, organ transplants, vaccinations, surgery, etc. . . . If we let "mother nature" work we would be all dead around 45 and 9 out of ten babies would die as infants . . .

8. "Only God can create life": this is pure belief, and religious people who are

against human cloning have the right and the freedom not to do it, as they can refuse blood transfusion, organ transplant, surgeries, antibiotics, contraception, abortion, etc., but those who decide to do it should be respected as well.

Curing Diseases and Spurring Discoveries

These are the most frequent objections to human cloning, but we should also consider the advantages in the middle and long term aspects of human cloning for a non-fanatically religious society.

Human cloning will help cure numerous if not all diseases. It will also make [it] possible to create a genetic bank where you will be able, if you need an organ transplant, to have it. Not by creating babies to take replacement organs from them . . . but by preserving stem cells of your body in very early stage embryos of yourself and develop[ing] in vitro only the organs you need in case of disease or accident . . . [T]hose opposed for religious reasons . . . should be free not to use it.

Finally, in the more long term, human cloning will make [it] possible—when Accelerated Growth Process [is] discovered to clone an adult copy of ourself directly just before we die and when Brain Data Transfer [is] discovered, to transfer, or download (or upload) our memory and personality in this new young body for a new long life. The progress of humanity will be exponential at this level. Presently, when a scientist is at the top of his art, he starts to age and dies. We can imagine Einstein, Newton and Leonardo Da Vinci still alive and working together . . . the discoveries they could do would be unlimited. And the same for artists like Mozart, Beethoven and Bach being still alive.

Not only should human cloning be allowed for the good of today's people, but even more for future generations who will remember your historical decision forever.

That's why I chose America to create the first Human Cloning company, because it is the country of individual freedom and science on earth. Thanks to the U.S. system, which should be a model for the whole world, and special thanks to the Supreme Court, I am confident that the right to clone yourself as an individual freedom, guaranteed by the great U.S. Constitution, will be protected.

Genetic Testing Raises Serious Ethical Concerns

by Shelley Burtt

About the author: *Shelley Burtt is a writer and a professor of political science who has taught at Yale University and the London School of Economics and Political Science.*

What sort of life is worth living? Advances in medical technology have given Socrates' question a new, more poignant meaning. For the first time in history, we have the means to will the disappearance of those born disabled at the same time that we have the resources to enable these children to live better and longer lives than was ever possible before. How will we respond to these new cross-cutting possibilities? Genetic testing gives us the tools to choose in advance against certain sorts of lives. How are these tools to be used? What sort of lives are worth living?

As a bereaved parent of a child with Down syndrome, I am painfully aware that the life my son led for two and a half joyous years is a life that many individuals would cut short before it began. Although genetic testing is often presented as a service designed to reassure parents that their children-to-be are without congenital abnormalities, the practice in fact functions to prescreen "defective" fetuses for abortion. The assumption of most health care providers in the United States is that the successful diagnosis of a genetic anomaly provides an opportunity to "cure" a pathological condition. Once the arrival of a normally healthy baby is in doubt, the decision to abort is seen as rational and the opportunity to do so as fortunate.

For an anxious parent, genetic testing accompanied by the possibility of therapeutic abortion appears to enhance individual freedom by providing an additional measure of control over one's reproductive choices. But this perspective represents a woefully limited understanding of what it might mean to live as or with a person whose genetic makeup differs markedly from the general popula-

Shelley Burtt, "Which Babies?: Dilemmas of Genetic Testing," *Tikkun*, vol. 16, January/February 2001, pp. 45–47. Copyright © 2001 by the Institute for Labor and Mental Health. Reproduced by permission of *Tikkun*: A Bimonthly Jewish Critique of Politics, Culture & Society.

tion and in a way that will to some extent impair his functioning. I'd like instead to explore what reasons we might have to resist the conclusion that a diagnosis of genetic abnormality is in itself a good reason to terminate a pregnancy and what cultural resources might be required to encourage this resistance.

A Personal Experience

My husband and I first welcomed Declan into our lives on a hot summer morning in July 1993. We had just come from the midwives' office where I had refused the genetic test (AFP) that screens for neural tube defects and would almost certainly have alerted us to our son's chromosomal abnormalities. Sitting on a bench outside Central Park, we asked ourselves, "What if there were a disability?" What use would we make of the information the test promised to provide? Although we come from different religious traditions (my husband is Jewish; I am Christian), we shared the view that the decision to create another human being was not conditional on the sort of human being that child turned out to be. For both of us, the child I was carrying was best understood as a gift we were being asked to care for, not a good we had the responsibility or right to examine for defects before accepting. With a blissfully innocent optimism, or perhaps an eerie prescience, we affirmed that day that we would love this child for who he was, whatever that turned out to be.

Not every couple will willingly go through a pregnancy in ignorance of their fetus's health or future prospects, especially when the tests for a variety of disabling conditions are so readily available. What we can insist on, however, is a clear-eyed recognition of how genetic testing actually functions in our society and a greater commitment on the part of medical practitioners and prospective parents to fully reflect on the knowledge it provides. Whether or not to carry on with a pregnancy at all, let alone one which will result in the birth of a child with either moderate or profound disabilities, ought to be a decision made carefully and thoughtfully by the prospective parents of that child, not by strangers, legislators, or disability rights activists. But what does a good decision in these circumstances look like?

For many bioethicists, the watchword when it comes to difficult decision-making is individual autonomy. The role of the medical practitioner is not to prescribe a course of action but to provide the necessary information for the patient to decide what he or she truly wants to do. Yet, when a fetus is diagnosed as disabled or "defective"

> *"To offer a therapeutic abortion as a 'cure' for [a] diagnosed disability is deeply disingenuous."*

in some way, few parents are offered a truly informed choice about their options, as medical providers are rarely neutral when it comes to choosing between bringing an abnormal fetus to term or ending the pregnancy and "trying again." Because genetic abnormality is defined not as one characteristic with which a human being might be challenged but as a treatable medical problem, few parents faced with a positive diagnosis are invited to think beyond the now troubled pregnancy to the joys and rewards as well as the heartache and challenge that accepting and raising a child with special needs can bring.

Helping Parents Raise Disabled Children

More than this: to offer a therapeutic abortion as a "cure" for the diagnosed disability is deeply disingenuous. We do not cure cystic fibrosis or Down syndrome by ensuring that fetuses carrying this trait do not come to term; we simply destroy the affected entity. The service health care providers offer in this regard is more truthfully characterized as a form of eugenics, either medical (if driven by physicians' preferences) or personal (if driven by parents'). Physicians genuinely-committed to patient autonomy in the context of genetic testing would not prejudge the worth or desirability of bearing a child whose genetic makeup was in some way abnormal. Instead, they would seek to ensure that parents truly understood what it meant to care for a child with special needs. This would mean, at a minimum, encouraging parents to inform themselves about the diagnosed condition, giving them the opportunity to speak to pediatricians familiar with the problem, and enabling them to meet with families already caring for children with this condition.

Those who believe that the practice of genetic testing followed by selective abortion is an acceptable way of ensuring the birth of a healthy child often argue that the desire to parent a

> *"The lives of those whose capacities fall outside the normal range must be personally and socially recognized as independently valuable."*

certain sort of child is not morally blameworthy. We can wish to be parents without wishing to be parents of a child with Fragile X syndrome or Tay-Sachs disease. Yet few who make this argument are willing to probe how our reproductive desires are constructed or at what point our desires become sufficiently self-reflective to be valid guides to action. On what basis do parents feel themselves "not ready" to parent a child with unexpectedly special needs? The picture they hold of a child's disabling trait and the effect it will have on the child and the family's life as a whole may be grounded in a volatile combination of fear and ignorance, not in some acquaintance with the actual life experiences of individuals already engaged in this task or deep reflection on the nature and purpose of parenting. It also seems likely that we cannot accurately assess in advance what challenges we are ready for. It is difficult to predict how we might grow and change in the face of seemingly adverse circumstances.

Certain parents might feel they cannot responsibly continue a pregnancy in which an abnormality has been diagnosed because they lack the financial or emotional resources to care for such a child. But this assessment is not made in a vacuum. What we feel we can manage depends in part on the level of social and political support families with disabled children can expect to receive, support which in turn depends on the degree to which such lives are valued or appreciated by our community.

Disabled Children Must Be Valued

The weight it is appropriate to give to parental desires in a reproductive context can perhaps be clarified by considering the internationally prevalent practice of sex-selective abortions. Parents around the world currently use the information derived from prenatal sonograms to advance their desire for a son by aborting female fetuses, a practice about which many physicians and most ethicists have grave moral reservations. Here, where parental desires are already considered suspect, the cultural construction of these desires and the appropriateness of resisting their expression is readily acknowledged. It is held to be an important part of making the world more just to change those cultural scripts which lead parents to prefer a son over a daughter so strongly that they will end a pregnancy rather than have a girl. We need to think critically and courageously about why a similar revaluation of social attitudes towards congenital disabilities is not also considered necessary.

I believe it is possible for some parents, after profound and prayerful reflection, to make the difficult decision that, all things considered, it is best for a child that it never be born. Incapacitating physical or mental deformity or the certainty of a life destroyed by a wasting disease are conditions which might conceivably, but not necessarily, call forth such a conclusion. But a judgement of this sort cannot be made with any fairness when speaking of disabilities such as spina bifida or Down syndrome where the quality of life available to the afflicted person is relatively high. A commitment to truly informed choice would ensure that we do not dismiss the possibility of caring for children burdened by disease or disability without an effort to appreciate and understand their possible lives.

But we need more than a commitment to truly informed choice if we are to create a world in which the birth of a disabled child is not thought of primarily as a stroke of bad luck, readily avoidable by more aggressive prenatal testing. The lives of those whose capacities fall outside the normal range must be personally and socially recognized as independently valuable, not only worth living in themselves but worth living with.

As the parent of a disabled child. I have experienced first hand the transformed perspective on life possible when one is given the opportunity to live with those who confound our routine expectations, who have too much or too little of a range of expected human traits, who experience life in a way that must remain opaque to the majority of normally functional human beings. What my parents' generation would have called Declan's "mental retardation," we termed his "developmental disabilities." But what was neither retarded nor disabled was an infectious enthusiasm for life which illuminated any interaction with him, an ability to give and receive love that was uncomplicated by the egoism, self-awareness, or self-consciousness of a "typical" child. Parenting this child forced us to reconsider our conception of what qualities and capacities made life worth living; the joy my son clearly took in life and the joy he gave us compelled such a re-evaluation.

But it is not enough to catalog the ways in which life with "them" is valuable for what it brings "us." The respect due to all persons by virtue of their humanity is not dependent on possessing only that sort of genetic makeup which guarantees normal human functioning. Our religious and political traditions teach that each human life has independent and intrinsic value. What would the consequences be of taking this truth seriously when we contemplated becoming parents?

Troubling Moral Decisions

Such a commitment would have to call forth a profound reassessment of the place of human will in the creation of human life. Both the cause of human freedom and of human equality have been admirably served by the ability, achieved only in this century, to choose to become parents. But we in the industrialized world now teeter on the brink of being able to choose what sort of children we want to become parents of. To some this capacity to control our destiny as parents is an almost unadulterated positive. One of the advantages of scientific progress is supposed to be the ability it gives humans to control their lives.

"We need . . . to rethink our willingness not only to live with the disabled but to live with unchosen obligations."

Some make the point that being a good parent is hard enough without the additional burdens of severe or moderate disabilities to cope with. Others argue that it is cruel to bring a child into the world who will always be different, for whom the normal trials of life will be magnified hundreds of times. Why not, then, embrace the opportunity offered by advances in prenatal testing to discard those reproductive efforts we will experience as "disappointing," less than perfect, abnormal, or unhealthy? The most important reason is that sorting the results of the human reproductive process in this way ranks human beings according to their capacity to please their creators, fulfill their parents' dreams, or contribute to social productivity. This willingness to sit in judgement over the sorts of persons deserving a place in our moral communities chases down rather than enlarges the scope of human freedom. The ability to control one's destiny that science supposedly promotes turns out to be conditional on being the right sort of person.

As my younger sisters became pregnant in the wake of Declan's death, I hoped right along with them for a niece or nephew free from illness, defect, or developmental challenges. The question is not whether it is right to desire a "normal" child, but how one ought to respond when genetic testing reveals that desire has been thwarted. To take steps at that point to abort the fetus and "try again" is not just to decide against being pregnant or in favor of "controlling one's life." It is to decide in advance and for another that a certain sort of life (a female one, a physically handicapped one, a mentally retarded one) is not worth living. The moral scope and impact of this decision appears to me far more troubling than a decision for or against parenthood based solely on a positive pregnancy test. Postponing an abortion decision until one knows what sort of child has been created places relative weights on human beings: some are more worthy of living, of being cared for, of being cherished, than others.

Having cared, however briefly, for a special needs child, I do not belittle the level of care and commitment called forth by the opportunity to parent a child or adult with moderate to severe disabilities. But I remain deeply skeptical that the best response to these challenges is the one currently favored by the Western medical establishment: to treat congenital imperfections as we do infectious diseases and to seek their cure by their eradication. Rather we need, through a genuine encounter with those whose identities are shaped but never fully encompassed by their bodies' imperfections, to rethink our willingness not only to live with the disabled but to live with unchosen obligations. Our cultural assumptions to the contrary, living a good and rich life does not require and is not identical with complete control of its circumstances. In fact, the aspiration for such "freedom" dishonors a fundamental aspect of the human condition. To those willing to recognize the essential humanity of every possible child, sometimes to choose not to know—or not to act on what we do know—will be the best choice of all.

Sex Selection Is Not Ethical

by Rebecca L. Riggs

About the author: *Rebecca L. Riggs is a staff member of the Concerned Women for America, a public policy organization that promotes biblical values.*

"A Boy or a Girl—You Choose." This slogan could soon be appearing at fertility clinics near you. Previously unheard of in the medical community, sex selection of embryos, for non-medical purposes, could begin in the next few days or weeks. In a story that seemed like science fiction, the *New York Times* reported on September 28 [2001] that Dr. Norbert Gleicher of the Center for Human Reproduction (CHR) said that the center would soon allow sex selection to provide "gender variety" to families.

In a press release dated September 27, CHR announced that it would begin to offer sex selection of embryos created for in-vitro fertilization through pre-implantation genetic diagnosis (PGD). This procedure screens embryos for their X & Y chromosomes and divides them by sex. Only those of the preferred sex would be implanted; the other tiny human beings would be discarded. This procedure is used already to prevent the passing of genetically sex-linked diseases, but now it could be used for non-medical reasons, namely a couple's personal preference.

Not an Approved Method

The center, according to Dr. Gleicher, believed its decision was based on the approval of the ethics committee of the American Society for Reproductive Medicine (ASRM), the body that sets ethical standards for fertility clinics across the country. But since the appearance of the *New York Times* article, ASRM has claimed that the letter merely expressed the opinion of John Robertson, the chairman of the ethics committee, and does not represent the opinion of the ASRM.

ASRM maintains the position that since May 2001 they have approved sperm sorting and other methods of preconception gender selection for non-medical reasons. Since sperm sorting happens before conception, it does not involve taking lives, as PGD does. ASRM specifies that the preconception methods are still experimental, and they should only be used to achieve "gender variety" in a family, meaning only parents with children of one sex should be able to seek to have children of the opposite sex. ASRM still stands behind a 1999 report that PGD for non-medical purposes, such as sex selection, should be discouraged.

> *"Sex selection is the first step down a road we have only looked at in science fiction, a road to designer human beings."*

According to Dr. Gleicher, CHR felt that this ruling "let the genie out of the bottle." If experimental types of preconception gender selection were ethical, then that which is 100-percent effective should be ethical as well, allowing for PGD for sex selection, he claimed. Dr. Gleicher told the NYT, "How can you say that a method that would be 100-percent reliable is not ethically acceptable?"

A Disregard for Life

Concerned Women for America can say Dr. Gleicher's 100-percent effective method is unethical because it destroys the embryonic children of the undesired sex. If parents want a girl, the boy embryos are discarded, then the girls are implanted in the mother's womb. CHR has assigned the personal preferences of parents a higher value than the lives of children. This shows an obvious disregard for life and turns a child into a pawn for the gratification of parents' wishes.

"Medical ethics boards are getting out of hand. They are becoming the puppets of the companies that pay them," said Wendy Wright, Director of Communications for Concerned Women for America. "The CHR decision to offer sex selection is driven by self interest, not principle. CHR will profit immensely as couples are given the opportunity to purposely dispose of children they don't want because of their sex."

This turns the argument to two even broader ethical dilemmas. The first is the legitimacy of any procedure of sex-selection. In China and India, newborn girls are already the targets of abuse and even murder. Under tight restrictions of population controllers, and the traditional desire for a male heir in these cultures, many mothers have seen infanticide as their only option after delivering a baby girl.

Until now, the Western world has demonized this atrocity. But if we make exceptions for our own version of the same procedure, we will also be guilty of infanticide. Sex selection via in-vitro fertilization makes the process less messy, but it still necessitates the killing of undesired children.

Commodifying Lives

Even if we are able to perform sex selection without killing children at the embryonic stage, through processes like sperm sorting, as ASRM has approved, we will still have crossed a terrible line of turning little lives into commodities, products to be designed and purchased. If we really have no problem with parents choosing the sex of their child, then why not her hair or eye color, IQ or special talents? To respect life, we have to honor the unique process through which it is created. A baby is a unique new life, not a newly designed product off the assembly line.

Sex selection is the first step down a road we have only looked at in science fiction, a road to designer human beings. Society still agrees that this is not a destination we want to reach, so we must not let the first step become an acceptable one.

Reproductive Technologies Should Not Be Federally Funded

by Leon R. Kass

About the author: *Leon R. Kass is a professor and the chairman of the President's Council on Bioethics.*

Should we allow or encourage [research into fertility] . . . [I] doubt the wisdom of proceeding with these practices, both in research and in their clinical application, notwithstanding that valuable knowledge might be had by continuing the research and identifiable suffering might be alleviated by using it to circumvent infertility. To doubt the wisdom of going ahead makes one at least a fellow traveler of the opponents of such research, but it does not, either logically or practically, require that one join them in trying to prevent it, say, by legal prohibition. Not every folly can or should be legislated against. Attempts at prohibition here would seem to be both ineffective and dangerous—ineffective because impossible to enforce; dangerous because the costs of such precedent-setting interference with scientific research might be greater than the harm it prevents. To be sure, we already have legal restrictions on experimentation with human subjects, restrictions that are manifestly not incompatible with the progress of medical science. Neither is it true that science cannot survive if it must take some direction from the law. Nor is it the case that all research, because it is research, is or should be absolutely protected. But it does not seem to me that *in vitro* fertilization and growth of human embryos or embryo transfer deserve, at least at present, to be treated as sufficiently dangerous for legislative interference.

But if doubting the wisdom does not oblige one to seek to outlaw the folly, neither does a decision to permit require a decision to encourage or support. A researcher's freedom to do *in vitro* fertilization, or a woman's right to have a child with laboratory assistance, in no way implies a public (or even a private)

Leon R. Kass, *Life, Liberty and the Defense of Dignity: The Challenge for Bioethics.* San Francisco: Encounter Books, 2002. Copyright © 2002 by Leon R. Kass. All rights reserved. Reproduced by permission of the publisher, Encounter Books, San Francisco, CA. www.encounterbooks.com.

obligation to pay for such research or treatment. A right *against* interference is not an entitlement *for* assistance. The question repeatedly debated from 1975 through 2001 was not whether such research should be permitted or outlawed, but only whether the federal government should fund it.

I propose to discuss this policy question here, and at some length, not because it is itself timely or relatively important—it is neither—but because it is exemplary. Policy questions regarding controversial new biomedical technologies and practices—as well as other morally and politically charged matters on the border between private and public life (for example, abortion, racial discrimination, developing the artificial heart, or affirmative action)—frequently take the form of arguments over federal support. Social control and direction of new developments is often given not in terms of yes or no, but rather, how much, how fast, or how soon? Thus, much of the present analysis can be generalized and made applicable to other specific developments in the field and to the field as a whole.

Pro-Research Arguments

The arguments in favor of federal support are well known. First, the research is seen as continuous with, if not quite an ordinary instance of, the biomedical research that the federal government supports handsomely; roughly one-half of the money spent on biomedical research in the United States comes from Uncle Sam. Why is this research different from all other research? Its scientific merit has been attested to by the normal peer review process of NIH (National Institutes of Health). For some, that is a sufficient reason to support it.

Second, there are specific and highly desired practical fruits expected from the anticipated successes of this new line of research. Besides relief for many cases of infertility, the research promises new birth control measures based upon improved understanding of the mechanisms of fertilization and implantation, which in turn could lead to techniques for blocking these processes. Also, studies on early embryonic development hold forth the promise of learning how to prevent some congenital malformations and certain highly malignant tumors (for example, hydatidiform mole) that derive from aberrant fetal tissue. Most important, research with embryonic stem cells and other more developed embryonic tissues offers great hope for treatment of many serious chronic diseases and disabilities, ushering in a new era of "regenerative medicine."

Third, as he who pays the piper calls the tune, federal support would make easy federal regulation and supervision of this research. For the government to abstain, so the argument runs, is to leave the control of research and clinical application in the hands of greedy, adventurous, insensitive, reckless or power-hungry private physicians, scientists or drug companies, or, on the other hand, at the mercy of the vindictive, mindless and superstitious civic groups that will interfere with this research through state and local legislation. Only through federal regulation—which, it is said, can follow only with federal funding—

will we have reasonable, enforceable and uniform guidelines.

Fourth is the chauvinistic argument that the United States should lead the way in this brave new research, especially as it will apparently be going forward in other nations. Years ago, one witness testifying before the Ethics Advisory Board that was charged to advise HEW [Department of Health, Education and Welfare] regarding federal funding of *in vitro* fertilization research deplored the fact that the first test-tube baby was British and not American. He complained, in effect, that the existing moratorium on federal support had already created what one might call an "*in vitro* fertilization gap." Similar arguments were heard during the stem cell funding debate in 2001. The preeminence of American science and technology (and commerce!), so the argument implies, is the center of our preeminence among the nations, a position that will be jeopardized if we hang back out of fear.

Not Vital Research

Let me respond to these arguments, in reverse order. Conceding—even embracing—the premise of the importance of science for American strength and prestige, it is far from clear that failure to support *this* research would jeopardize American science. Certainly the use of embryo transfer to overcome infertility, though a vital matter for the couples involved, is hardly a matter of vital national interest—at least not unless and until the majority of American women are similarly infertile. The demands of international competition, admittedly often a necessary evil, should be invoked only for things that really matter; a missile gap and an embryo transfer gap are chasms apart. In areas not crucial to our own survival, there will be many things we should allow other nations to develop, if that is their wish, without feeling obliged to join them. Moreover, one should not rush into potential folly in order to avoid being the last to commit it.

> "*Federal research funds targeted for the relief of infertility should certainly go first to epidemiological and preventive measures.*"

The argument about governmental regulation has much to recommend it. But it fails to consider that there are other safeguards against recklessness, at least in the clinical applications, known to the high-minded as the canons of medical ethics and to the cynical as liability for malpractice. Also, federal regulations attached to federal funding will not in any case regulate research done with private monies, for example, by the drug companies. Moreover, there are enough concerned practitioners of these new arts who would have a compelling interest in regulating their own practice, if only to escape the wrath and interference of hostile citizens' groups in response to unsavory goings-on. Organized professional societies have and will issue guidelines for their members, and the prestige of membership keeps even the more adventurous from violating the norms. The available evidence does not convince me that a sensible practice of *in vitro* experimentation requires regulation by the federal government.

In turning to the argument about anticipated technological powers, we face difficult calculations of unpredictable and more-or-less likely costs and benefits, and the all-important questions of priorities in the allocation of scarce resources. Here it seems useful to consider separately the techniques for generating children, the anticipated techniques for birth control or for preventing developmental anomalies and malignancies, and studies that could usher in the great age of regenerative medicine.

First, accepting that providing a child of their own to infertile couples is a worthy goal—and it is both insensitive and illogical to cite the population problem as an argument for ignoring the problem of infertility—one can nevertheless question its rank relative to other goals of medical research. One can even wonder whether it is indeed a *medical* goal, or a worthy goal for medicine, that is, whether alleviating infertility, especially in this way, is part of the art of healing. Just as abortion for genetic defect is a pecu-

> *"Much as I sympathize with the plight of infertile couples, I do not believe they are entitled to the provision of a child at public expense."*

liar innovation in medicine (or in preventive medicine) in which a disease is treated by eliminating the patient (or, if you prefer, a disease is prevented by "preventing" the patient), so laboratory fertilization is a peculiar treatment for oviduct obstruction in that it requires the creation of a new life to "heal" an existing one. All this simply emphasizes the uniqueness of the reproductive organs in that their proper function involves other people, and calls attention to the fact that infertility is not a disease, like heart disease or stroke, even though obstruction of a normally patent tube or vessel is the proximate cause of each.

Focus on Preventive Measures

However this may be, there is a more important objection to this approach to the problem. It represents yet another instance of our thoughtless preference for expensive, high-technology, therapy-oriented approaches to disease and dysfunctions. What about spending this money on discovering the causes of infertility? What about the prevention of tubal obstruction? We complain about rising medical costs, but we insist on the most spectacular and the most technological—and thereby often the most costly—remedies.

The truth is that we do know a little about the causes of tubal obstruction, though much less than we should or could. For instance, it is estimated that at least one-third of such cases are the aftermath of pelvic inflammatory disease, caused by that uninvited venereal guest, gonococcus. Leaving aside any question about whether it makes sense for a federally funded baby to be the wage of aphrodisiac indiscretion, one can only look with wonder at a society that will have "petri-dish babies" before it has found a vaccine against gonorrhea.

True, there are other causes of blocked oviducts, and blocked oviducts are not the only cause of female infertility. True, it is not logically necessary to choose between prevention and cure. But *practically* speaking, with money for research as limited as it is, federal research funds targeted for the relief of infertility should certainly go first to epidemiological and preventive measures—especially where the costs of success in the high-technology cure are likely to be great.

The Costs of Research

What about these costs? Let us, for now, consider only the financial costs. How expensive is a baby produced with the aid of *in vitro* fertilization? Hard to say exactly. To the costs of hormone preparation of ovaries and uterus, laparoscopy, fertilization and growth *in vitro*, and transfer, one must add the costs of closely monitoring the baby's development to check on her "normality" and, should it come, the costs of governmental regulation. And then there are the costs of failure and having to try again. A conservative estimate places the costs of a successful pregnancy of this kind between $10,000 and $15,000. If we use the conservative figure of 500,000 for estimating the number of infertile women with blocked oviducts in the United States whose *only* hope of having children lies with *in vitro* fertilization, we reach a conservative estimate cost of $5 to $7.5 billion. Is it fiscally wise for the federal government to start down this road?

Clearly not, if it is also understood that the costs of providing the service, rendered possible by a successful technology, will also be borne by the taxpayers. Nearly everyone now agrees that the kidney machine legislation, obliging the federal government to pay for kidney dialysis for anyone in need, is an impossible precedent—notwithstanding that individual lives have been prolonged as a result. But once the technique of *in vitro* fertilization and embryo transfer is developed and available, how should the baby-making be paid for? Should it be covered under medical insurance? If a national health insurance program is enacted, will and should these services be included? (Those who argue that they are part of medicine will have a hard time saying no.) Failure to do so will make this procedure available only to the well-to-do, on a fee-for-service basis. Would that be a fair alternative? Perhaps, but it is unlikely to be tolerated. Indeed, the principle of equality—equal access to equal levels of medical care— is the leading principle in the press for medical reform. One can be certain that efforts will be forthcoming to make this procedure available equally to all, independent of ability to pay, under Medicaid or national health insurance or in some other way. (A few years ago, an egalitarian Boston-based group concerned with infertility managed to obtain private funding to pay for artificial insemination for women on welfare!)

Much as I sympathize with the plight of infertile couples, I do not believe they are entitled to the provision of a child at public expense, especially now, especially at this cost, especially by a procedure that also involves so many moral difficulties. Given the many vexing dilemmas that will surely be spawned by laboratory-assisted reproduction, the federal government should not be misled by compassion to embark on this imprudent course.

In considering the federal funding of such research for its other anticipated technological benefits, independent of its clinical use in baby-making, we face a more difficult matter. In brief, as is the case with all basic research, one simply cannot predict what kinds of techniques and uses it will yield. But here, also, I think good sense would at present say that before one undertakes human *in vitro* fertilization to seek new methods of birth control (for example, by developing antibodies to the human egg that would physically interfere with its fertilization) one should make adequate attempts to do this in animals. One simply can't get sufficient numbers of human eggs to do this pioneering research well—at least not without subjecting countless women to additional risks not to their immediate benefit. Why not test this conceit first in the mouse or rabbit? Only if the results were, very promising—and judged also to be relatively safe in practice—should one consider trying such things in humans. Likewise, the developmental research can and should be first carried out in animals, especially in primates. Purely on scientific grounds, the federal government ought not *now* to be investing its funds in this research for its promised technological benefits—benefits that, in the absence of pilot studies in animals, must be regarded as mere wishful thoughts in the imaginings of scientists.

Feminists' Support of Reproductive Technologies Is Misguided

by Christine Stolba

About the author: *Christine Stolba is a fellow at the Ethics and Public Policy Center.*

To invoke Prometheus, the figure of Greek myth who was punished by Zeus for stealing fire from Hephaestus and giving it to humans, has become a popular warning against scientific hubris in our new age of biotechnology and genetic engineering. But the second half of the Promethean myth offers a further warning: Prometheus's defiant act led Zeus to dispatch a woman, Pandora, to unleash her box of evils on the human race—and thus eliminate the power differential that access to fire briefly had given mankind.

A New and Dangerous Power

Pandora's box of dark arts is an apt metaphor for human reproductive technologies. Despite being hailed as important scientific advances and having succeeded in allowing many infertile couples to have children, the next generation of these technologies offers us a power that could prove harmful to our understanding of what motherhood is. This new generation of reproductive technologies allows us to control not merely the timing and quantity of the children we bear, but their quality as well. Techniques of human genetic engineering tempt us to alter our genes not merely for therapy, but for enhancement. In this, these technologies pose moral challenges that are fundamentally different from any we have faced before.

Contemporary human reproductive technologies range from the now widely accepted practice of in-vitro fertilization (IVF), where physicians unite egg and sperm outside the woman's body and then implant the fertilized egg into the womb, to sophisticated sex selection techniques and preimplantation genetic diagnosis of disease and disability in embryos. Today, for-profit clinics, such as Conceptual Options in California, offer a cafeteria-like approach to human reproduction with services such as IVF, sex selection screening, and even "social surrogacy" arrangements where women who prefer not to endure the physical challenges of pregnancy rent other women's wombs. New techniques such as cytoplasmic cell transfer threaten to upend our conceptions of genetic parenthood; the procedure, which involves the introduction of cytoplasm from a donor egg into another woman's egg to encourage fertilization, could result in a child born of three genetic parents—the father, the mother, and the cytoplasm donor—since trace amounts of genetic material reside in the donor cytoplasm. Doctors in China recently performed the first successful ovary and fallopian tube transplant, from one sister to another, which will allow the transplant recipient to conceive children—but from eggs that are genetically her sister's, not her own.

The near future will bring uterus transplants and artificial wombs. Scientists at Cornell University are perfecting the former, while researchers at Juntendou University in Tokyo, who have already had success keeping goat fetuses alive in artificial wombs for short spans of time, predict the creation of a fully functional artificial womb for human beings in just six years. Cloning technologies eventually could fulfill even the most utopian of feminist yearnings: procreation without men via parthenogenesis, something that excited the passions of Simone de Beauvoir in 1953. "Perhaps in time," she mused in *The Second Sex*, "the cooperation of the male will become unnecessary in procreation—the answer, it would seem, to many a woman's prayer."

De Beauvoir was correct to identify women's hopes as a powerful force in modern challenges to old-fashioned procreation, but these hopes also pose serious ethical challenges. Contemporary feminism's valorization of "choice" in reproductive matters and its exaltation of individualism—powerful arguments for access to contraceptives and first-generation reproductive techniques—offer few ethical moorings as we confront these fundamentally new technologies. In fact, the extreme individualism of the feminist position is encouraging women to take these technologies to their logical, if morally dubious conclusion: a consumer-driven form of eugenics.

Lacking an Ethical Foundation

Our biotech era has exposed a serious contradiction in feminist thinking: Feminists want women to maintain absolute control over reproductive decisions, but thus far their arguments have rested on a feeble hope that women will not choose to do detrimental things. They have failed to construct a plausible and stable ethical basis upon which to make morally sound decisions about human reproductive technologies. The feminists' approach to gene therapy for the purposes of enhancement, for example, is little different from their stance on plastic surgery—we are told that it does not serve women's best interests but are given no ethical guidance on the elimination of these incorrect desires. What happens when women, as avid consumers, exercise that control and use sperm sorting to give birth only to sons, or as their justification for genetically manipulating their children?

The triumph of individual choice as an unassailable right also prevents us from engaging in important debates about the broader social implications of reproduction and the technologies that promise to change its meaning. Drawing the delicate line between genetic therapy and enhancement is a difficult task, and quality of life a malleable concept. Recently, a woman with a history of early-onset Alzheimer's disease paid a fertility clinic to screen her IVF-created embryos for the defective gene, discard the embryos that were found to have it, and implant a "clean" embryo that did not carry the genetic marker. Is this eugenics, preventive therapy, or simply the neutral exercise of individual choice?

> *"[Feminists] have failed to construct a plausible and stable ethical basis upon which to make morally sound decisions about human reproductive technologies."*

The desire to control reproduction and conquer biology was a central part of the feminist-driven political and sexual revolutions of the late twentieth century. In her 1970 manifesto, "The Dialectic of Sex," radical feminist Shulamith Firestone wrote that the "first demand" of a feminist social order would be "the freeing of women from the tyranny of their reproductive biology by every means available." In their push to populate classroom, courtroom, and boardroom, feminists implicitly endorsed Firestone's goal, securing the contraceptive and abortion rights they saw as crucial for women's advancement in the public realm. Feminism insisted that women try to overcome, or at least willfully ignore, biological realities.

By the late twentieth century, the feminist movement's effort to liberate women from reproduction had produced unexpected results. A majority of women routinely used birth control, accepted abortion as a right, and viewed IVF and other first-generation reproductive technologies as useful tools of last resort for the infertile. But the women who embraced the feminist message about reproduction—the daughters of the sexual revolution—eventually felt that message's sting personally. They found themselves entering middle age with ripe careers but declining fertility. Today they form a large portion of the fertility industry's customers, spending tens of thousands of dollars for a single chance to cheat time. The facts are stark: According to a January 2002 report on aging and infertility in women, published by the American Society for Reproductive Medicine, a woman's fertility begins to decline in her late twenties and drops precipitously around the age of 35. Although fertility experts quibble over precise odds, there is a consensus that by the time a woman is in her forties, her odds of having a child, even with some form of intervention, are less than 10 percent. For these women, reproduction is not the tyranny imagined by Firestone, but an unfulfilled hope. A recent educational campaign launched by the American Infertility Association and the American Society for Reproductive Medicine is directed at the daughters of this feminist generation; fertility specialists hope to combat the undue optimism of women in their twenties and thirties about their ability to have children as they get older.

As the controversy—and, in some quarters, consternation—that greeted Sylvia Ann Hewlett's recent book, *Creating a Life: Professional Women and the Quest for Children*, revealed, we are still uncomfortable, as a society, with airing too many of these facts about fertility. Hewlett, who gently rebukes women for assuming that the fertility industry could extend their reproductive lives long enough for them to make partner (and chastises the fertility industry for insinuating that it could), nevertheless is herself wary of trampling the principle of choice. Instead, in interviews with childless women that speak poignantly to the intractability of biology, Hewlett uncovers something called "creeping non-choice," a condition treatable, in her view, with a strong dose of government social policy and more "intentional" plotting by women of their reproductive futures.

What Hewlett and others overlook is a different and more disturbing facet of "choice," the one that inexorably pulls us toward making "intentional" decisions about the *kind* of children we have. The sentiment is already gaining the sanction of clinical practitioners. A recent study conducted by University of Massachusetts public health professor Dorothy Wertz and University of Virginia bioethicist John Fletcher revealed that 62 percent of American geneticists would agree to perform sex-selection tests on fetuses (or refer them to specialists who would) for parents who stated ahead of time their desire to have an abortion if the fetus was the "wrong" sex. In the early 1970s, a similar study found that only 1 percent of physicians and ethicists would do the same.

The Feminist View of Science

If clinicians are less inclined to question the limits of individual choice in these matters, our self-appointed ethical guides in the field of bioethics should. In fact, the burgeoning field of bioethics now supports a subdiscipline in feminist bioethics, with its own organizations and methodological assumptions and with a keen interest in reproductive technologies. Unfortunately, feminist bioethicists remain wedded to a misguided view of science and medicine as inherently biased against women, and they pursue a feminist worldview that applauds "difference" but offers few limits on the excessive individualism that is the logical conclusion of their emphasis on choice in reproductive matters.

Although resting along various points of the ideological spectrum, feminist bioethicists share certain core principles—most important, a concern that human reproductive technologies are being developed in the context of a society that has not yet granted women full equality. The International Network on

Feminist Approaches to Bioethics, a consortium launched in 1992, is "committed to a non-hierarchical model of organization" and takes as its goal the development of "a more inclusive theory of bioethics encompassing the standpoints and experiences of women and other marginalized social groups." The group's mission statement also includes a vow to deconstruct "presuppositions embedded in the dominant bioethical discourse that privilege those already empowered."

> *"Feminist bioethicists remain wedded to a misguided view of science and medicine as inherently biased against women."*

In this, feminist bioethics has its roots in broader feminist critiques of both science and ethics, two enterprises they view as inherently masculine and biased. Critics such as Lynda Birke of the University of Warwick and Sandra Harding of the University of California, Los Angeles, have argued for a "feminist science" that rejects objectivity in favor of intuition and seeks to supplant Francis Bacon's metaphor of Mother Nature as a "common harlot" meant to be tamed and molded by men with more inclusive practices. Their critique of science has trickled down into popular culture through narratives, such as Naomi Wolf's *Misconceptions*, that attack the male medical establishment for its treatment of pregnant women, and through manuals such as the popular alternative feminist health book, *Our Bodies, Ourselves*, which has been in print continuously since 1970.

The feminist critique of ethics is also intent on illuminating women's subordination. As feminist bioethicist Rosemarie Tong of the University of North Carolina notes, feminist ethicists "ask questions about male domination and female subordination *before* they ask questions about good and evil, care and justice, mothers and children." Moreover, women's subordination "leads to women's disempowerment morally and personally as well as politically, economically, and socially." This twin focus on women's disempowerment and the masculine bias of science serves an important exculpatory purpose—as ethical escape hatches—in the field of feminist bioethics.

Autokoenomy Has Chilling Effects

The current reigning principle in bioethics is autonomy, which grants to individuals the freedom to choose for themselves what they want to do until they begin to infringe on the liberty of others or cause serious harm. Feminist bioethicists promote something different; they endorse the principle of "autokoenomy," from the Greek for self (*auto*) and community (*koinonia*). As Tong notes, "unlike the autonomous man who thinks that his self is entirely separable from others . . . the autokoenomous woman realizes that she is inextricably related to other selves." The implication is that autokoenomy fosters a humility that is otherwise lacking in strict autonomy, since it emphasizes a person's place in a particular community, or an "epistemology of perspective."

In practice, autokoenomy appears to foster confusion, not ethical guidance. As an ethical principle, it appears to allow nearly any ethical choice, including eugenic choices, as long as the choice is made in the service of gender equity. "It is to be hoped," Tong writes, "that women will choose the characteristics of their fetuses in ways that will break down gender inequity and the host of other human oppressions to which it is related. In choosing for their fetuses, women will be choosing for themselves." Laura Purdy, of the University of Toronto, is another feminist bioethicist who approves of genetic screening for the purpose of weeding out the unfit; she declares "unjustifiable" the "rejection of so-called quality control that uses genetic services to prevent the birth of babies at risk for serious physical or mental illness or disability." Since women are primary caregivers to children, Purdy reasons, their autonomous interests are infringed upon when those children are burdened by genetic conditions that require more devoted parental care. Purdy concludes that failing to prevent the birth of a child with serious defects is "immoral."

Autokoenomy can also begin to resemble a chilling utilitarian "community" of one. University of Chicago feminist bioethicist Mary Mahowald draws on the "ethics of care" and "maternal thinking" models of Carol Gilligan and Sara Ruddick to promote a "feminist standpoint theory" that parallels Rosemarie Tong's autokoenomy. Mahowald's feminist standpoint theory endorses women having babies for the explicit purpose of harvesting spare parts for themselves or loved ones. The ethic on which she relies would "support a decision to become pregnant in order to provide the [fetal] tissue to someone with whom one has a special relationship." Moreover, Mahowald says, "a pregnant woman might herself be the recipient and could deliberately become pregnant in order to provide the fetal tissue that might lead to her own cure." As Tong and Mahowald's reasoning reveals, autokoenomy has little to say about the excesses of individual choice.

Fear of Male Control

At the other end of the spectrum are feminist bioethicists who do not so eagerly embrace reproductive and genetic technologies, although they do share with their autokoenomous sisters a devotion to feminist politics. As Tong says, "all feminist approaches to bioethics share a common methodology—namely, the methodology of feminist thought." But feminist principles make for an awkward fit in the field of bioethics, for in focusing so keenly on science's patriarchal bias, feminist critics of reproductive technologies miss the most serious challenges these new tools pose.

Australian feminist Robyn Rowland has been issuing warnings since the early 1980s about the dangers of male control of reproductive technologies. Men have "coveted" the power women have over reproduction, Rowland argues. "Now, with the possibilities offered by technology they are storming the last bastion and taking control of conception, fetal development, and birth." But this is only part of a larger control men exercise over women, according to Rowland's critique. "Being the dominant social group, men expect to control all social resources, including reproduction," Rowland argues. They "use the vehicles of science, medicine and commerce to establish control over procreation." Men, Rowland concludes, are making women into "patriarchy's living laboratories."

Another feminist critic of reproductive technologies, former *New York Times* reporter Gena Corea, assails as "propaganda" the notion that women should procreate. It is patriarchal society that pushes this pronatalism, Corea argues, and it "has a coercive power." "It conditions a woman's choices as well as her motivations to choose," she says, leaving her incapable of rendering an authentic ethical choice about her reproductive options. Janice Raymond, a feminist theorist who teaches at the University of Massachusetts, has argued that new reproductive technologies might be used by the patriarchal medical establishment as a tool for the "previctimization" of women, eliminating or fundamentally altering females before they are even born. "Technological reproduction is brutality with a therapeutic face," Raymond avers. In 1984, some of the more earnest skeptics of reproductive technologies organized FINRRAGE—Feminist International Network of Resistance to Reproductive and Genetic Engineering—a small group that hosts conferences to raise awareness of the dangers of these new interventions.

Genetic technologies are also viewed with suspicion by feminists who fear they will undermine feminism's valorization of "difference." Maura Ryan, a professor of Christian Ethics at Notre Dame University, has argued that genetic technologies are "at odds with a feminist view of community where all are welcome and persons are challenged to deal creatively with difference." Yet arguments for difference can take unexpected twists, as they did recently when they were invoked by a deaf lesbian couple in Bethesda, Maryland, who used sperm donated by a fifth-generation deaf man to ensure that their son and daughter would be born profoundly deaf. Since the women view deafness not as a disability, but as a sign of membership in a specific cultural community, they wanted to guarantee that their children would be part of that community as well.

What these feminist skeptics of reproductive technologies share is an assumption, guided by feminist politics and feminist critiques of science, that women lack control over even the most rudimentary reproductive decisions. This leaves them unwilling to tackle thorny ethical practices, such as sex selection, that rest on women's own choices. Evidence from China and India indicates that women in those countries avidly rid themselves of female fetuses, usually by making use of ultrasound machines and abortion, creating a serious imbalance in male-to-female sex ratios in the process. In the United States, sex selection is gaining in popularity, with new techniques such as sperm sorting offered by many fertility clinics.

Sex Selection and Eugenics

Feminists have a stock answer when questioned about the use of sex selection in countries such as India and China: Blame the sin, not the sinner. Because these women are living in undemocratic, patriarchal societies, they are eligible for feminist bioethicists' ethical escape hatch. "The solution is not to take away abortion rights," a spokesperson for the group Population Action International stated, "but rather to elevate the status of women so that the economic and cultural incentives for sex-selection abortion are no longer there." This rationale is less compelling when applied closer to home, where feminist claims of patriarchal control do not ring true. Bioethicist Mary Mahowald suggests that "selection of either males or females is justifiable on medical grounds and morally defensible in other situations so long as the intention and the consequences are not sexist." But how does one judge whether consequences are sexist? In the United States, many women use sex selection to have girls. "Women are the driving force, and women want daughters," one fertility doctor told the *New York Times* in 1999.

> *"Our new reproductive future ... suggests a society where male responsibility and fatherhood take on a different form."*

Even mainstream feminist groups, such as the National Organization for Women, conveniently ignore incorrect expressions of choice. NOW has no official position on the use of sex-selective ultrasound and abortion or other sex-selection techniques, yet the group did endorse a resolution at its national conference last year [2001] calling for the protection of the rights of "intersex girls" (girls born with atypical sexual anatomy). The resolution, which called on parents to resist imposing hormone treatments and surgery on their daughters until the daughters themselves could choose whether or not they wanted to become fully female, was deemed part of the organization's "movement for reproductive freedom and bodily integrity."

Although feminist bioethicists have failed to come to terms with the impulse to control the quality of one's offspring, especially among women, it is not a new one. In Spartan society, women were responsible for bearing sons who would be formidable warriors and for rigorously weeding out those who would not, leaving them to die of exposure in the chasm called the *Apothetae*. In the mid-nineteenth-century utopian community of Oneida in upstate New York, it was women more than men who eagerly volunteered for leader John Humphrey Noyes's proto-eugenic experiments in breeding better children—an undertaking he likened to plant breeding and called "human stirpiculture." During the heyday of the American eugenics movement, as historian Wendy Kline has found, women's reform organizations were some of the most enthusiastic lobbyists for compulsory state sterilization laws meant to combat the menace of the so-called feebleminded. Women embraced an ideal of "scientific" and "responsible" motherhood that emphasized the quality of the children being born, and found in the eugenic impulse to "improve the human race through better breeding" a compelling justification for their efforts.

The birth control movement of the early twentieth century offers perhaps the most extended case study of this impulse. In her 1920 polemic, "Woman and the New Race," birth control activist Margaret Sanger described how "millions of women are asserting their right to voluntary motherhood. They are determined to decide for themselves whether they shall become mothers, under what conditions, and when." But the logic of that assertion encompassed more than control of quantity. Like many of her peers, Sanger shared her culture's desire for eugenic "race improvement." Fearful that the vaunted American melting pot was no longer assimilating new waves of immigrants from southern and eastern Europe, Sanger argued that contraception could alleviate the burden of bad stock. "Birth control, often denounced as a violation of natural law," she wrote, "is nothing more or less than the facilitation of the process of weeding out the unfit, of preventing the birth of defectives, or of those who will become defectives." The "voluntary motherhood" Sanger pursued had as its goal the "creation of a new race" and drew upon the language of choice and the individual rights of women to achieve it.

Many of Sanger's more astute contemporaries understood the radical nature of the new ideal of motherhood she was promoting. In *A Preface to Morals*, Walter Lippmann urged society to consider the "full logic of birth control," which he saw as making parenthood a "separate vocation," detached from the "hard realities" and ambiguities of life and thus ultimately "efficient, responsible, and dull." Birth control is like the automobile, Lippmann argued, capable of hurtling us along at terrifying speeds to new and exciting destinations, but a device whose "inherent possibilities do not fix the best uses to be made of it."

Our Reproductive Future

Today our devices are more numerous and powerful, but contemporary feminist bioethicists remain mired in the individualistic rhetoric of the previous era's technologies and politics. The end pursued by feminist bioethicists is an egalitarian feminist society, but they assume that this society would consist of feminist mothers choosing traits for their children that conform to "women's values." In this, feminist ethicists betray the fact that they have not strayed far from the utopian yearnings of their foremothers. Charlotte Perkins Gilman's 1915 feminist utopian novel *Herland* found perfection in a world where men did not exist and where parthenogenic births produced only girl children; contemporary fiction writer Marge Piercy's 1976 novel, *Woman on the Edge of Time*, offered a similar social vision. In Piercy's world, citizens of the utopian society of Mattapoisett decide that to end sexism, classism, and racism, reproduction must be removed from the control of one particular sex. "It was part of women's long revolution," one of Piercy's characters explains. "As long as we were biologically enchained, we'd never be equal. And males never would be humanized to be loving and tender. So we all became mothers. Every child has three. To break the nuclear bonding."

We are not all mothers yet, but if we continue along the path our feminist ethical guides have laid down, we run the risk of ending up in a consumer-driven eugenic society. With ever more sophisticated IVF techniques, genetic screening, and artificial wombs, the physiological process of pregnancy and childbirth could become just another commodified "life experience." Like climbing Mt. Everest or meditating on an ashram, seekers of the exotic could experience the "adventure" of childbirth the old-fashioned way, while some women would make use of artificial wombs to avoid the hassles of pregnancy.

Our new reproductive future also suggests a society where male responsibility and fatherhood take on a different form. Shotgun weddings and social stigmas that used to keep men close to their offspring have disappeared, but in an age where embryos are stored in fertility clinics like jewelry in safe deposit boxes, men have begun to claim paternal rights using the language of property. Popular culture has enlisted science to help them. Producers of daytime talk shows are leavening the sensationalism of their broadcasts with paternal "outings" using DNA tests; men who suppose themselves the father of a child are told, on-air in front of a studio audience and their wayward partners, that DNA tests have proven otherwise.

We are being eased into this bread-and-circuses world of reproduction by the very rhetoric that once promised to free women from the burdens of biology: the rhetoric of choice that feminists have long championed. Choice will allow us to begin crossing the line between genetic therapies and genetic enhancements—quietly at first, but eventually with ease. Genetic engineering could become just another reproductive right. But this normalization process comes with a cost that first-generation technologies such as IVF never posed: altering the human race and, in the process, fating for extinction biological motherhood as we have known it. With feminist principles guiding us and a public preternaturally optimistic about and desirous of new reproductive technologies, Pandora has met Dr. Pangloss.[1] But all is *not* for the best in this best of all possible worlds.

One would hope that, having had glimpses of the logical conclusion of their principles, feminists would make a well-timed retreat from their glorification of choice in reproductive matters. Such a retreat is unlikely, however, for making it would require feminists finally to concede that there is no such thing as "women's values" or the sisterhood for which they have served as self-appointed spokeswomen. Such a retreat would force feminists to confront the fact that some women make ethically unsound choices not because they are victims of male domination, but because they lack ethical moorings, and it would require them to recognize that in a world of unfettered individualism, women's choices will not lead to a feminist vision of women's liberation.

1. a character in the book *Candide*

Human Reproductive Cloning Is Not Ethical

by Michael R. Soules

About the author: *Michael R. Soules is a professor of obstetrics and gynecology and the director of the Division of Reproductive Endocrinology and Infertility at the University of Washington in Seattle.*

Since the birth of Dolly the sheep in 1997, both the scientific world and the general public have become fascinated with the concept of cloning. There are different types of cloning, as detailed below:

1. *Reproductive cloning:* Somatic-cell nuclear transfer into an enucleated oocyte followed by creation of an embryo that is transferred into a receptive uterus for the purpose of creating a pregnancy.

2. *Therapeutic cloning:* Somatic-cell nuclear transfer into an enucleated oocyte followed by development of an embryo that is never transferred. Therapeutic cloning is done to derive stem cells from the cloned embryo that are antigenically identical to the somatic cell donor and manipulated to develop immunologically compatible replacement tissue.

3. *Embryonic cloning:* Creation of an embryo by standard IVF [in vitro fertilization] techniques with enucleation of the blastomeres and transfer of those nuclei into oocytes from the same species, followed by embryo development. These derived embryos are all identical and when transferred into a recipient uterus will lead to pregnancy and delivery of identical offspring. This technique has been used in monkeys and other species to create a relatively small subset of identical siblings for research. To my knowledge, no one is promoting use of embryonic cloning in human reproduction.

What has caught the attention of the general public, the news media, and the U.S. Congress is the potential for human reproductive cloning. While some have speculated that human reproductive cloning has already been attempted, no documentation supports that contention. However, [in 2000 and 2001], two different groups have called press conferences to announce their intention to do reproductive cloning in humans. These announcements culminated in a Congressional hearing on March 28, 2001, at which I represented the American Society for Reproductive Medicine (ASRM). In this editorial, I wish to clarify the ASRM's position on human reproductive cloning.

Cloning Is Not Safe

The success of reproductive cloning depends on the species. We come into contact with plant cloning every day—for example, an apple comes from a cloned fruit tree. Cloning in small animal species, such as the mouse, has been reasonably efficient. However, reproductive cloning in large domestic animal species has been fraught with problems. In such animals as the sheep, cow, goat, and pig, few embryos are formed from somatic-cell nuclear transfer, the embryo implantation rate is very low, the spontaneous abortion rate is high, as are the rates of fetal mortality and congenital anomalies. Placental malfunction has frequently been described, as have respiratory distress and circulatory problems in offspring who survive to term. At the Congressional hearing, Mark E. Westhusin, Ph.D., associate professor in the Department of Animal Science at Texas A&M University, testified that

> In cattle, approximately 90% of the fetuses produced by cloning die and abort between days 35 and 90 of gestation. The most common developmental malformation observed to date is aberrant placentation. These placental abnormalities pose serious health risks not only to the developing fetus and offspring but also to the surrogate mothers carrying the pregnancies. In several cases involving cattle, both the surrogate mother and the bovine fetuses have died during late gestation due to a variety of complicated health issues related to the abnormal pregnancy. Moreover, even if the cloned offspring survive to term, many of the resulting calves exhibit developmental abnormalities and die at birth or shortly thereafter, usually as a result of cardio-pulmonary abnormalities.

Reproductive cloning therefore appears to be neither efficient nor safe in higher animal species.

To my knowledge, reproductive cloning has not been attempted in nonhuman primates. In medical science, the proper order of animal experiments leading to human trials is to proceed from a rodent model to a mammalian model to a nonhuman primate model to humans. Since reproductive cloning is neither acceptably efficacious nor safe in domestic mammals, it is not yet time to proceed to monkeys, let alone humans. It would be totally irresponsible to attempt human reproductive cloning based on the current state of this art.

Three Unacceptable Arguments

After listening closely to the testimony of the two groups in favor of attempting human reproductive cloning, now their arguments to proceed with this unproven technology fell into three categories; reproductive freedom, freedom of scientific inquiry, and patient demand.

In the United States, a consensus toward reproductive freedom extends from the Supreme Court to Congress to the general public. Reproductive decisions, from whether a couple wishes to remain childless or want to use donor gametes to achieve pregnancy, are respected and supported in the medical and legal community. It is intuitively obvious (yet often overlooked) that reproduction by nature includes a third party—the child. Reproductive freedom can only be respected in the context of reasonable medical safety for mother, father, *and* child.

Freedom of scientific inquiry is also generally supported in the United States, but cannot be honored when there are significant safety issues. Would Neil Armstrong have been sent to the moon if there had been greater than 90% chance that he would not survive?

The final argument for pursuing human reproductive cloning at this time— patient demand—is the most unaceptable. Infertile patients are often desperate and therefore, vulnerable; in my experience, they often do not make good decisions. Anyone who justifies reproductive cloning on the basis of requests from infertile patients is pandering to a vulnerable audience.

Reproductive Cloning Is Unethical

The ASRM Ethics Committee published an ethical statement on reproductive cloning in the November 2000 issue of [*Fertility and Sterility*]. The Ethics Committee carefully analyzed the arguments for and against reproductive cloning. They pointed out that cloning would represent a major clash of reproductive freedom with prevalent social values. The Committee concluded that human reproductive cloning per se is ethically uncertain and its eventual application should be preceded by a thoughtful discussion among individuals, health care providers, religious organizations and government. However, the unanimous and firm opinion of the Committee is that human reproductive cloning is unethical at this time because of safety concerns. Before public debate can begin, reproductive cloning needs to be as safe as other accepted fertility treatments.

> *"Reproductive cloning . . . appears to be neither efficient nor safe in higher animal species."*

The ASRM is the largest and most influential professional society devoted to the practice and advancement of reproductive medicine. Our members include not only physicians from multiple specialties but also basic scientists, clinical embryologists, nurses, mental health professionals, clinic managers, and attorneys. Because the ASRM's membership is diverse, many different opinions have been voiced on the human application of reproductive cloning. In that sense, ASRM does not have a position on reproductive cloning. If or when cloning is shown to be efficacious and safe, the ASRM will reconsider its position.

The ASRM considers human reproduction cloning unethical at this time because of safety issues. Although the ASRM is against cloning, it supports cloning for basic and clinical research in animals, therapeutic cloning and stem-cell research, discussion and debate within its ranks, and reproductive freedom.

The Role of the Government

The role of the U.S. Food and Drug Administration (FDA) in regards to reproductive cloning remains controversial. In 1998, the FDA sent letters to most assisted reproductive technology programs, stating that the FDA had jurisdiction over human reproductive cloning. In testimony before Congress, Kathryn C. Zoon, Ph.D., of the FDA claimed that

> The use of cloning technology to clone a human being would be subject to both the biologic provisions of the Public Health Service [PHS] Act and the drug and device provisions of the Federal Food, Drug, and Cosmetic [FD&C] Act. Before such clinical research could begin, the researcher must submit an Investigational New Drug [IND] request to the FDA, which the FDA would review to determine if such research could proceed.

However, at the Congressional hearing, the Chairman of the House Energy and Commerce Committee, Representative W.J. "Billy" Tauzin (R-LA), as well as an attorney/witness, expressed skepticism that the FDA had authority under Federal law to regulate embryo research and reproductive cloning. They indicated that the FDA was stretching

"Cloning would represent a major clash of reproductive freedom with prevalent social values."

to try to include reproductive cloning under the PHS [U.S. Public Health Service] or FD&C [Federal Food, Drug, and Cosmetic Act] act. The FDA's authority in this area has never been tested in court.

The ASRM supports the FDA requirement to submit an IND [investigational new drug application] for any reproductive cloning research in humans. We encourage all of our members to comply with FDA guidelines. However, the only consideration that is of statutory concern to the FDA is safety. If or when reproductive cloning is shown to be medically safe in higher animal species, the FDA's concerns will be answered and human reproductive cloning will be permissible. Congress expressed concern that safety considerations alone are not sufficient, and that cloning should be debated on an ethical level before it is allowed in the United States.

A Potential Violation of the Hippocratic Oath

Assisted reproductive technology represents a unique field in which medical practice and laboratory science intimately collaborate in providing medical care. The basic scientist/embryologist in an assisted reproductive program is an integral part of the medical team and properly shares the rewards (building families) and responsibilities of the physician members of the team. In that sense, the Hippocratic Oath which, in essence, states, "Do no harm" applies to laboratory staff as well as medical personnel. The potential to do irrevocable harm is clearly present with the current state of reproductive cloning technology. Neither an ethical medical practitioner nor an ethical basic scientist/embryologist should undertake this challenge. Human reproductive cloning undoubtedly represents a major scientific hurdle. The lay press has depicted the technology as relatively simple in the context of a functioning ART [assisted reproductive technology]. In truth, reproductive cloning is extremely inefficient in animal models and human application would require a vast outlay of time and money even among physicians and scientists with ample IVF [in vitro fertilization] experience. However, inefficiency in itself is not a valid argument against pursuing human reproductive cloning—IVF itself was inefficient 20 years ago when it was first applied to humans.

In conclusion, ASRM supports advances in reproductive medicine but finds human reproductive cloning unethical at this time owing to safety concerns. Whenever a major new therapy is first considered (e.g., bone marrow transplantation) providers tend to have strong opinions (bias) both for and against full human application. Thus, there is need to protect patients who may be harmed by premature or poorly designed medical trials designed by biased investigators. The medical/scientific community supports the human subject review process when medical advancements are introduced, and ASRM considers it unconscionable to bypass it in any proposed attempts at human reproductive cloning.

Chapter 4

Are Genetic Technologies Ethical?

Chapter Preface

Stem cell research and other genetic technologies have the potential to provide cures for many deadly and debilitating diseases, including cancer and Alzheimer's. One procedure which holds promise is gene therapy, in which genetic ailments are potentially cured via the insertion of normal or genetically altered genes into patients' cells. While several gene therapy experiments have shown promise, the harm that the procedure has caused to some patients raises serious questions about the safety and ethics of gene therapy.

Several hopeful results have emerged from gene therapy. Although some studies are still at their early stages, there are indications that combining gene therapy with other techniques, including radiotherapy, can help fight cancer. Clinical trials on Alzheimer's patients have shown that gene therapy, in this case using modified skin cells to introduce a nerve growth factor into the brain, can slow down the progress of the disease for at least two years.

However, gene therapy has also been accompanied by serious, and even fatal, complications. On September 17, 1999, eighteen-year-old Jesse Gelsinger died during a gene therapy experiment when the adenovirus—a virus that causes respiratory diseases—that transported genetic material into his body caused his immune system to overreact. Gelsinger suffered from blood clotting, respiratory disease, and liver and kidney failure for four days before he died. A French gene therapy trial on eleven boys who were born without a working immune system was halted in early 2003 when two of the boys developed leukemia. Similar experiments in the United States were also aborted following that revelation. Problems such as these have prompted calls for bans on gene therapy. Critics of the procedure include the American Association for the Advancement of Science, which argues that the negative effects of gene therapy might not be fully known for many generations.

David A. Dean and R. Allen Perkin, writing for *American Family Physician*, sum up the challenges facing gene therapy: "While gene therapy may be to the 21st century what antibiotics were to the last, we have a long way to go before success is at hand. . . . However, as with all discoveries and new fields, problems do exist, and they need to be identified, studied and overcome." Concerns about the ethics and safety of gene therapy will either lead to a heightened desire to solve these problems, in order to ensure that future clinical trials will be safe, or to a slowing down (and possible elimination) of the procedure altogether.

While the future of gene therapy is unclear, genetic technologies as a whole are one of the most important topics in the modern medical ethics debate. The authors in this chapter evaluate the moral consequences of cutting-edge medicine.

Cloning Can Enhance Lives

by Robert W. Tracinski

About the author: *Robert W. Tracinski is the editor and publisher of the* Intellectual Activist.

On July 31, [2001] The House of Representatives voted overwhelmingly for a ban on human cloning—a ban so sweeping that it threatens to wipe out whole areas of genetic research. According to a *Los Angeles Times* summary:

> The penalties make participation in human cloning in any way—from creating cloned cells to patients receiving medicine based on such research done abroad—subject to a felony conviction that could bring a 10-year prison term and, if done for profit, civil penalties of more than $1 million.

To justify threatening scientists, doctors, and patients with ten-year prison terms, anti-cloning activists ought to be able to project some kind of disastrous consequence that would flow inevitably from this technology. Here is the best they have been able to offer.

Parents, anti-cloning activists say, could create children who are exact copies of themselves, and then attempt to live vicariously through their cloned children. But how is this different from what some parents already do with the inexact copies of themselves created the old-fashioned way?

Drawing on science-fiction fantasies, activists also claim that cloning would be used to create a genetic "underclass"—or, alternately, a genetic "overclass." In fact, cloning *per se* would create genetic copies of people who already exist, whose progeny would be no more or less gifted, and have no more and no fewer privileges, than the originals.

Anti-cloning activists also claim that the existence of genetically identical clones will cause a "loss of individuality"—a fear which, if it were true, ought to make us abhor identical twins. But it isn't, and we don't.

Unreasonable Fears

These arguments don't add up. As [author and philosopher] Harry Binswanger points out, none of this can "account for the virtual panic over human cloning, nor for the fact that the anti-cloning clique opposes human cloning across the board, in any quantity, for any reason." The opposition to cloning, he concludes, "springs from something primordial, the fear of the unknown, the fear captured in the catch-phrase: 'We can't play God.'"

A clue to this primordial fear is, ironically, the frequent invocation of scenarios borrowed from science fiction. Wisconsin Republican James Sensenbrenner, chairman of the House Judiciary Committee, embodied this approach when he called cloning a "new brave world of Frankenstein science." Sensenbrenner is the only person, so far, who has managed to combine in one sentence the cloning debate's two omnipresent science-fiction bogeymen: Aldous Huxley's turgid eugenics fable *Brave New World*, about a future society divided into genetically distinct classes, and Mary Shelley's *Frankenstein*, in which a mad scientist grasps the secret of creating life and uses it to create a monster.

The common theme of these literary works is that too much science and technology—too much human control over nature—is dangerous. That is the intellectual theme echoed by opponents of cloning. Just as Mary Shelley's mad scientist warned, "learn from . . . my example how dangerous is the acquirement of knowledge, and how [miserable is] he who aspires to become greater than his nature will allow"—so Leon Kass, a University of Chicago professor and "medical ethicist," warns against "the Frankensteinian hubris to create human life and increasingly to control its destiny; man playing at being God."

Kass is one of the most prominent—and most intellectual—opponents of cloning. Human procreation, he writes, should consist of surrendering to the "lottery of sex," of "relinquishing our grip" on nature and "saying yes to . . . the limits of our control." In keeping with this view, Kass even opposes *in vitro* fertilization, the "test-tube" method used to help infertile couples have children. His perspective is captured by the distinction he makes between "making" or "manufacturing" a child and "begetting" one. The use of the Biblical term is no accident; his argument consists of a sophisticated mysticism, a superstitious awe of the "natural order" allegedly ordained by God.

This outlook was echoed in the . . . congressional debate by House Majority Whip Tom DeLay: "[Cloning] would reduce some human beings to the level of an industrial commodity. It is an exploitative, unholy technique that is no better than medical strip-mining."

Surrendering to Nature

The arch-conservative's derogatory references to industrial commodities and strip-mining reveal his common ground with the other religious group that opposes cloning: environmentalists. The radical greens also believe in surrendering passively to Mother Nature, their god. Again, the fictional examples are revealing. Just as Huxley's *Brave New World* idealized the life of the few "Savages" remaining on the "Reservation"—so environmentalists glamorize the way of life of Stone-Age Indians. Yes, they say, we should have no cloning—and we should also have no genetically engineered "Frankenfoods," no animal testing, no modern farming, no roads, no automobiles, no power plants, no computers, no suburban homes.

The environmentalists take the injunction not to "play God" to its logical conclusion. As Dr. Binswanger observes, "A surgeon 'plays God' whenever he removes a cancer or an infected appendix rather than letting the patient die. We 'play God' anytime we use our intelligence to improve the natural course of events. . . . Not to 'play God' in this way means to abandon the struggle for human life and submit uncomplainingly to whatever happens." Yet that is precisely what the greens propose.

> *"The lives that could be saved by [cloning] number in the millions."*

Brave New World and *Frankenstein* serve as symbols used to transmit this anti-mind, anti-human philosophy to the public on a sense-of-life level, without having to state or defend that philosophy in fully explicit terms. In clamoring about the dangers of a "brave new world," the anti-cloning forces implicitly admit that they want to send us back to a timid old world—a world of primitive savages shivering passively in caves.

But these fictional references also serve another purpose. Invoking examples from science fiction excuses the anti-cloning activists from having to confront real-life science fact.

Cloning Research Is Beneficial

Here, for example, is the most important and promising area of actual cloning research. Scientists are attempting to take genetic material from the cell of a living patient and clone it by injecting it into an unfertilized egg cell. As the egg divides and becomes an embryo, it produces "stem cells," a kind of master cell capable of producing any kind of tissue in the human body. Scientists hope to discover how to harness these stem cells to grow replacement tissues, ranging from new skin for burn victims to new hearts, livers, and spleens for transplantation; because these new organs are genetically identical to the originals, they would escape rejection by the body's immune system.

The benefit for those who now die while waiting for a transplant, or who suffer the debilitating side-effects of anti-rejection drugs, is incalculable. The lives that could be saved by this technology number in the millions. But thanks to years of bombardment with science-fiction scare stories, opponents of this research expect the average person to regard it as eerie and ominous, as "unnatural" and "inhuman."

In reality, however, nothing could be *more* human. Man's mind is his tool of survival, his natural means of dealing with the world; everything he has is created through the effort of his mind. When man builds a fire, or invents a steam engine, or creates an artificial heart, or grows a cloned replacement organ, he is not "tampering with nature." He is being true to his nature.

This is the "brave new world" of science fact: a world in which man uses the highest faculties of his mind to prolong and enhance his life. We should demand the freedom to move bravely forward.

Embryonic Stem Cell Research Is Ethical

by Orrin G. Hatch

About the author: *Orrin G. Hatch is a Republican U.S. senator from Utah.*

Editor's Note: The following viewpoint was originally written as a letter to Health and Human Services Secretary Tommy G. Thompson. In August 2001 President George W. Bush ruled that embryonic stem cell research could be performed only on existing cell lines.

Dear Mr. Secretary:[1]
I am writing to express my views regarding federal funding of biomedical research involving human pluripotent embryonic stem cells. After carefully considering the issues presented, I am persuaded that such research is legally permissible, scientifically promising, and ethically proper.

Staunch Opposition to Abortion

At the outset, let me be clear about one of my key perspectives as a legislator: I am pro-family and pro-life. I abhor abortion and strongly oppose this practice except in the limited cases of rape, incest, and to protect the life of the mother. While I respect those who hold a pro-choice view, I have always opposed any governmental sanctioning of a general abortion on demand policy. In my view, the adoption of the Hyde Amendment wisely restricts taxpayer financed abortions. Moreover, because of my deep reservations about the Supreme Court's decision in *Roe v. Wade*, I proposed—albeit unsuccessfully—an amendment to the Constitution in 1981 that would have granted to the states and Congress the power to restrict or even outright prohibit abortion.

In 1992, I led the Senate opposition to fetal tissue research that relied upon cells from induced abortions. I feared that such research would be used to jus-

1. Secretary of Health and Human Services Tommy G. Thompson

Orrin G. Hatch, letter to Health and Human Services Secretary, Tommy G. Thompson, June 13, 2001.

tify abortion or lead to additional abortions. It was my understanding that tissue from spontaneous abortions and ectopic pregnancies could provide a sufficient and suitable supply of cells. Unfortunately, experts did not find these sources of cells as adequate for their research needs. . . .

I am proud of my strong pro-life, anti-abortion record. I commend the Bush Administration for its strong pro-life, pro-family philosophy. In my view, research on stem cells derived from embryos first created for, but ultimately not used in, the process of in vitro fertilization, raises questions and considerations fundamentally different from issues attendant to abortion. As I evaluate all these factors, I conclude that this research is consistent with bedrock pro-life, pro-family values. I note that our pro-life, pro-family Republican colleagues, Senators Strom Thurmond and Gordon Smith, as well as former Senator Connie Mack, support federal funding of embryonic stem cell research. It is my hope that once you have analyzed the issues, you will agree with us that this research should proceed.

The Benefits of New Technologies

While society must take into account the potential benefits of a given technological advance, neither scientific promise nor legal permissibility can ever be wholly sufficient to justify proceeding down a new path. In our pluralistic society, before the government commits taxpayer dollars or otherwise sanctions the pursuit of a novel field of research, it is imperative that we carefully examine the ethical dimensions before moving, or not moving, forward.

I would hope there is general agreement that modern techniques of in vitro fertilization are ethical and benefit society in profound ways. I have been blessed to be the father of six children and the grandfather of nineteen grandchildren. Let me just say that whatever success I have had as a legislator pales in comparison to the joy I have experienced from my family in my roles of husband, father, and grandfather. Through my church work, I have counseled several young couples who were having difficulty in conceiving children. I know that IVF [in vitro fertilization] clinics literally perform miracles every day. It is my understanding that in the United States over 100,000 children to date have been born through the efforts of IVF clinics.

Intrinsic with the current practice of IVF-aided pregnancies is the production of more embryos than will actually be implanted in hopeful mothers-to-be. The question arises as to whether these totipotent embryonic cells, now routinely and legally discarded—-amid, I might add, no great public clamor—should be permitted to be derived into pluripotent cells with non-federal funds and then be made available for research by federal or federally-supported scientists?

Stem Cells and Morality

Cancer survivor and former Senator, Connie Mack, . . . explained his perspective on the morality of stem cell research in a *Washington Post* op-ed piece:

It is the stem cells from surplus IVF embryos, donated with the informed consent of couples, that could give researchers the chance to move embryonic stem cell research forward. I believe it would be wrong not to use them to potentially save the lives of people. I know that several members of Congress who consider themselves to be pro-life have also come to this conclusion.

Senator Mack's views reflect those of many across our country and this perspective must be weighed before you decide.

Among those opposing this position is Senator [Sam] Brownback, who has forcefully expressed his opinion:

The central question in this debate is simple: Is the embryo a person, or a piece of property? If you believe . . . that life begins at conception and that the human embryo is a person fully deserving of dignity and the protection of our laws, then you believe that we must protect this innocent life from harm and destruction.

While I generally agree with my friend from Kansas on pro-life, pro-family issues, I disagree with him in this instance. First off, I must comment on the irony that stem cell research—which under Senator Brownback's construction threatens to become a changed issue in the abortion debate—is so closely linked to an activity, in vitro fertilization, that is inherently and unambiguously pro-life and pro-family.

> *"A frozen embryo is more akin to a frozen unfertilized egg or frozen sperm than to a fetus."*

I recognize and respect that some hold the view that human life begins when an egg is fertilized to produce an embryo, even if this occurs *in vitro* and the resulting embryo is frozen and never implanted *in utero*. To those with this perspective, embryonic stem cell research is, or amounts to, a form of abortion. Yet this view contrasts with statutes, such as Utah's, which require the implantation of a fertilized egg before an abortion can occur.

Not Akin to Abortion

[The question is] whether a frozen embryo stored in a refrigerator in a clinic is really equivalent to an embryo or fetus developing in a mother's womb? To me, a frozen embryo is more akin to a frozen unfertilized egg or frozen sperm than to a fetus naturally developing in the body of a mother. In the case of in vitro fertilization, extraordinary human action is required to initiate a successful pregnancy while in the case of an elective abortion an intentional human act is required to terminate pregnancy. These are polar opposites. The purpose of in vitro fertilization is to facilitate life while abortion denies life. Moreover, as Dr. Louis Guenin has argued: "If we spurn [embryonic stem cell research] not one more baby is likely to be born." I find the practice of attempting to bring a child into the world through in vitro fertilization to be both ethical and laudable and distinguish between elective abortion and the discarding of frozen embryos no longer needed in the in vitro fertilization process.

In evaluating this issue, it is significant to point out that no member of the United States Supreme Court has ever taken the position that fetuses, let alone embryos, are constitutionally protected persons. To do so would be to thrust the courts and other governmental institutions into the midst of some of the most private of personal decisions. For example, the use of contraceptive devices that impede fertilized eggs from attaching onto the uterine wall could be considered a criminal act. Similarly, the routine act of discarding "spare" frozen embryos could be transformed into an act of murder.

As much as I oppose partial birth abortion, I simply cannot equate this offensive abortion practice with the act of disposing of a frozen embryo in the case where the embryo will never complete the journey toward birth. Nor, for example, can I imagine Congress or the courts somehow attempting to order every "spare" embryo through a full term pregnancy.

Mr. Secretary, I greatly appreciate your consideration of my views on this important subject. I only hope that when all the relevant factors are weighed both you and President [George W.] Bush will decide that the best course of action for America's families is to lead the way to a possible new era in medicine and health by ordering that this vital and appropriately regulated research proceed.

Religious Arguments Against Embryonic Stem Cell Research Are Baseless

by Richard Dawkins

About the author: *Richard Dawkins is the Charles Simonyi Professor of Public Understanding of Science at Oxford University in England.*

Embryonic stem cell research was once billed as the defining issue of the second Bush's presidency. Things have moved on with a vengeance, but the issue, though no longer defining, has not gone away. If anything, Bush the victorious warlord seems likely to get an easier ride for his domestic policies than Bush the unelected Supreme Court appointee could ever have hoped for. Our vigilance must not waver.

Bush's weak compromise on stem cell research is still government policy, and it remains as confused as it was when he announced it on August 9, 2001.[1] Surplus embryos are routinely flushed down the drain in the majority of *in vitro* fertilization cycles. So, if stem cells are to be taken only from existing lines for fear of killing new embryos, IVF should be banned too. Of course it isn't, and it won't be. Nor should we expect funeral services and miniature gravestones for surplus conceptuses. That's all that needs to be said about that. I want to concentrate on another aspect, the capacity of religion to muddy the waters in such ethical disputes.

Biblical Reasoning

In the run-up to Bush's odd decision, both sides in the debate could be heard eloquently trading quotations from the Bible—as though that were any way to settle an argument. Notwithstanding the vaunted constitutional separation of

1. President George W. Bush stated that stem cell research would be limited to sixty then-existing "lines" of stem cells.

Richard Dawkins, "Homsap: Elixir of Holiness," *Free Inquiry*, vol. 22, Spring 2002, pp. 9, 12. Copyright © 2002 by the Council for Democratic and Secular Humanism, Inc. Reproduced by permission.

church and state, Congress resounded with "chapter and verse" like an old-style revival tent. Senator Gordon Smith (R-Ore.) is an opponent of abortion but a supporter of embryonic stem cell research, and he invoked Genesis 2:7: "And the Lord God formed man of the dust of the ground, and breathed into his nostrils the breath of life." What we have here, explained the resourceful senator, is a "two-step process" for creating humans (*Los Angeles Times*, July 19, 2001). The dust, in Step 1, clearly means cells. Step 2, in which God went for the nostril "and man became a living soul," obviously corresponds to implantation in the womb. So it's O.K. to do stem cell research, so long as the cells are taken before implantation.

Richard Doerflinger, spokesman for the National Conference of Catholic Bishops, criticized Senator Smith's "amateur theology." Well, it sounded pretty amateurish to me (though I can't help wondering what a "professional" theology could conceivably look like). What if one of Smith's opponents had offered a different reading of the symbolism of Genesis? Symbols are so nebulous and adjustable, how do you decide between them? What if yet another senator had riposted with a quote from the Qur'an, or the Bhagavad-Gita? Would they have been self-evidently less valid than the Bible? Who says? Whose holy book trumps? You can see why the Founding Fathers insisted on the separation of church and state.

Senator Sam Brownback (R-Kan.) was not to be outdone in theological close reasoning: "We all agree that the embryo is alive. The question is, is it a life?" Bush asked almost the identical question in his speech. It is a question that these people honestly think means something. Brownback took the view that stem cell research would deny "the dignity of the young human, effectively making the human embryo equal to mere plant or animal life or property." On the other side some theologians, including even some Catholic ones, have suggested that an embryo less than fourteen days old cannot be "a person" because before that age it is still capable of dividing and becoming two people. I can just hear an ambitious young theologian advance the opposite view: an early embryo is *twice* as valuable precisely because it is capable of becoming not one soul but two! Again, by what objectively defensible standards are theological arguments to be judged?

Perhaps seeking to beat the senators at their own biblical game, a spokesman for a Massachusetts company doing stem cell research quoted Matthew 25, the parable of the talents and the servants. Two of the servants, you will remember, put their gold talents to work and doubled their worth. The third one fearfully buried his, and was duly chided: "Thou wicked and slothful servant." The spokesman might have added that stem cell research will certainly go on apace with private funds—also, of course, in other well-

> *"Most reasonable thinkers would agree that an early human embryo suffers less than an adult cow or pig."*

equipped countries, and there are indications that some leading American researchers are already on the move. The prospect of a reverse brain drain delights Dr. Harry Griffin, deputy director of the Roslin Institute in Scotland, where Dolly [a sheep] was cloned.

The Confusion of Absolutism

"Do No Harm," an influential lobby of "pro-life" (read pro-*human* life) doctors and other medical professionals, has condemned all embryonic stem cell research. Let's hope, for their patients' sake, that these well-meaning doctors are better practitioners than they are thinkers. They are big on the dignity and status of the human embryo which, they are in no doubt, counts as a fully paid-up human individual. It "is human; it will not articulate itself into some other kind of animal. Any being that is human is a human being." And they unashamedly play the emotive cards of race, slavery, and Nazi atrocity:

> The last century and a half has been marred by numerous atrocities against vulnerable human beings in the name of progress and medical benefit. In the 19th century, vulnerable human beings were bought and sold in the town square as slaves and bred as though they were animals. In this century, the vulnerable were executed mercilessly and subjected to demeaning experimentation at Dachau and Auschwitz.

What is the connection with embryos? You may well ask. The chief confusion in the minds of these unrepresentative doctors is human absolutism, pinned down with famous clarity by Jeremy Bentham (1748–1832), founding father of utilitarian moral philosophy.

> . . . a full-grown horse or dog is beyond comparison a more rational, as well as a more conversable animal, than an infant of a day, or a week or even a month old. But suppose the case were otherwise, what would it avail? The question is not, can they reason? Nor can they talk? But, *can they suffer?*

You don't have to follow Bentham all the way to giving a horse or a dog human rights. But he should make you think hard about why you favor, by comparison, a microscopic ball of cells containing no nerves at all.

The same absolutism rang through Bush's statement of August 9. He was preoccupied with the sacredness of life, and he only occasionally bothered to make it explicit that by "life" he meant "human life": ". . . human life is a sacred gift from our Creator. I worry about a culture that devalues life." Cynics might like to note that the number of Texans Bush executed as governor exceeds the margin of votes by which he can claim to have won Florida [in the controversial 2000 presidential election].

Let's pick the confusion of the human absolutists apart. They start with the admirable principle that suffering is a bad thing, from which the vulnerable should be protected. Undeniably, slaves and victims of Nazi experiments suffered, and nothing like that should ever be allowed to happen again. Equally undeniably, those vulnerable victims were human. So far so good. The fallacy creeps in at the next stage. It does *not* follow that *all* vulnerable victims capable of suffering are human. Nor does it follow that all human entities are capable of suffering. To apply Bentham to a fertilized egg, the question is not, "Is it a member of a particular species, other members of which can suffer?" Nor "Is it potentially capable of turning into an individual (or even two individuals) which could suffer?" No, the relevant question is "Does this embryo, here and now as a cluster of cells, suffer?"

Only Humans Matter

Most reasonable thinkers would agree that an early human embryo suffers less than an adult cow or pig with its fully functioning nervous system. If you happen to be a vegan and an opponent of embryonic stem cell research, I salute your high principles and consistency. You really don't like things to suffer. But if you eat cows, as Bush surely does, yet still call yourself a pro-lifer because you oppose abortion and stem cell research, where is your consistency? Where is your logic? A Colorado beetle has a better claim to suffer than a human gastrula.

But of course the "pro-life" argument is not really about suffering at all. Pro-life, as I have already noted, has a hidden meaning: pro-*human* life. The embryos that pro-lifers seek to protect do not suffer, but they are infinitely precious simply and solely because they belong to the species *Homo sapiens*. Humanness is a mystical quality, something absolute and indivisible, something God-given . . . for of course this faulty reasoning all comes from religion, and only from religion.

It is here that the religious mind most starkly exposes its lamentable shortcomings. This kind of religious mind just knows, without question and without reason, that there is something self-evidently special about *Homo sapiens*, an essence of such infinite apartness that it overrides Benthamite questions like "Can they suffer?" or "Can they think?" It is as though we had a unique and magical substance called Homsap, an enchanted juice, a divine elixir that bathes every cell of *Homo sapiens* and of no other species.

Well, that may be appealing, but evolutionary biology tells us it is rubbish. No doubt *Homo sapiens* does have remarkable and even unique features, but these *emerge* from the *organization* of our trillions of cells, especially our brain cells, and from our shared cultural experiences. Infinite moral value is not baptized upon us by simple virtue of the species to which we belong. The essentialist view that humans are deeply special, down to their very substance, is profoundly at odds with the fact of evolution. But that must wait for another column.

Cloning Runs Counter to Christian Beliefs

by Amy Coxon

About the author: *Amy Coxon is a laboratory biologist at the Center for Cancer Research at the National Cancer Institute.*

"As things are, there is no reason to assume that anything we might reasonably conceive of doing with living tissues might not be possible; living tissues are proving to be remarkably compliant. . . . [We] can look forward to an age in which the understanding of life's mechanisms will be virtually total, that is, the principal systems will be understood molecule by molecule. From this total understanding will come—if we choose—total control. Of course the word 'total' is too absolute. There will always be deficiencies and inconsistencies. Biology will never come to an end. But for all practical purposes we might as well assume that absolute control will be possible. It is not irresponsible—nor, indeed, sensationalist—to suggest this. It is irresponsible to imply the opposite, that our power will always be too limited to worry about. We are entering the age of biological control, and we should gird our moral and political loins accordingly."

Understanding Therapeutic Cloning

The above quote from Ian Wilmut, the man who captured the world's attention with his creation of Dolly, the cloned sheep, should awaken us all to the vast power of the scientific community, as well as to the desire for total control held by so many scientists in this post-modern era.

Given the spin that science and the media have put on the latest achievement in medical science—the cloning of the first human embryo—some reading this [viewpoint] may truly believe that there are good, and even therapeutic, reasons for human cloning and that human cloning cannot really result in the development of a human being to the point of birth. This [viewpoint] is intended to help Christians gain an understanding of what therapeutic cloning really is and how it may be used to treat disease, as well as to equip them to evaluate their position on this issue by providing them with both an understanding of the science and the truths of Scripture as they relate to this technology.

Deceptive Terminology

First, there is absolutely no difference in the scientific techniques used to accomplish—or the embryonic human beings produced—via therapeutic cloning or the cloning of a human being for other purposes. The idea that an "organism" created by cloning is a "new type of biological entity never before seen in nature" is an attempt by scientists to hide the truth of this new technology behind scientific jargon. Instead of calling this cloned organism an embryo, which is precisely what it is, scientists have labeled it an "activated egg." This is again manipulation of terminology with the hope of deceiving the public. In fact, the term "therapeutic cloning" itself is used to deceive the general public into believing that human cloning is acceptable and beneficial in certain medical circumstances. With the media's and the scientific community's frequent misuse of scientific terminology, it is crucial that we as Christians correctly discern the meanings behind this terminology. If we do not take steps to understand the science, we cannot defend our position in an educated manner and therefore will have no public voice on these issues.

> *"The term 'therapeutic cloning' . . . is used to deceive the general public into believing that human cloning is acceptable and beneficial."*

All human cloning, whether "therapeutic" or not, is done in the following manner. First, scientists take DNA (deoxyribonucleic acid—the genetic material of most organisms) from any cell in the body that is not a germ cell (sperm or egg). The cells the DNA is taken from are called somatic cells. Somatic cells contain two copies of each of the genes that make up a person's DNA (diploid), while germ cells contain only one copy of each of the genes of a person's DNA (haploid). Diploid DNA from a somatic cell is then inserted into a human egg cell which has had its own DNA removed (enucleated). This process is known as somatic cell nuclear transfer (SCNT), because the nucleus of the somatic cell containing the diploid DNA has been transferred to an egg that has no nucleus. At the point of transfer, the egg becomes diploid, meaning it now contains two copies of the DNA necessary to code for a human being. It is now an embryo.

At this point, the question may be raised as to how an embryo is created without a sperm uniting with the egg. In the normal process of fertilization and embryo formation, the egg and sperm cells each have only one copy, or half, of the DNA necessary to code for a fully functioning human being. Each of these cells is haploid. When the sperm and egg unite, they form a cell with two copies of the total DNA necessary for a human being to develop (diploid). At the point of union of the sperm and egg, an embryo is created. The definition of fertilization is "the process of union of two gametes whereby the somatic chromosome number is restored and the development of a new individual is initiated." Scientifically speaking, then, the development of a new individual is initiated at the point of fertilization, when the somatic chromosome number is restored, thereby making a diploid fertilized egg (embryo).

Cloning Creates Human Life

As you can see by comparing the science, both "therapeutic" cloning and normal fertilization result in the production of an embryo. In the process of "therapeutic" cloning, the transfer of diploid DNA from a somatic cell into an enucleated egg results in the egg cell being made diploid (becoming an embryo) and the initiation of the development of a human being. In the process of fertilization occurring between an egg and a sperm, the egg is haploid (one copy of the DNA) and the sperm is haploid (one copy of the total DNA). The union of the egg and sperm forms a diploid cell, the embryo, which then divides en route to becoming a fully developed human being. In order for a normal human being to develop, an embryo must be diploid or contain two copies of each chromosome. In the cases of "therapeutic" cloning and natural fertilization, a diploid embryo is created so that "the somatic chromosome number is restored and the development of a new individual is initiated."

Scientists have made claims that an "organism" created by cloning is not human. In fact, members of Advanced Cell Technology's ethics advisory board have stated that, "Although it [a cloned human embryo] possesses some potential for developing into a full human being . . . it has no organs, it cannot possibly think or feel, and it has none of the attributes thought of as human." However, these statements are also equally true of a naturally created embryo in its earliest stages, which we know to be human. Indeed, it is well-known and well-documented in the scientific literature that cloned embryos of other species that are transferred at the embryo stage into the womb of a female and survive to birth are born as animals of the species to which they belong. That is to say, cloned mice have been born as mice, sheep as sheep, goats as goats, cattle as cattle, and pigs as pigs—not as "a new type of biological entity never before seen in nature." So, while scientists claim that the entity cloned from a human is "not really human," we can be certain that these claims are wrong based on recent cloning experiments with other species which have resulted in the birth of organisms of the same species from which they were cloned.

"Therapeutic" cloning, then, results in the creation of a human being. Scientists do not want to recognize this fact because recognizing these clones as humans would create more problems in using embryonic human clones for research purposes. At this point, "therapeutic" cloning of humans has failed to produce the coveted embryonic stem cells for use in research because, although scientists have claimed to clone the first human being, that human being died at the six-cell stage. In order to use cloned embryos for "therapeutic" purposes, they must live to about day six, when they contain hundreds of cells. However, if scientists are able to extend the survival of these cloned human beings, their stem cells could be obtained via the same destructive process used to obtain stem cells from "surplus" embryos created via in vitro fertilization (IVF). In both cases, the embryo is destroyed in culture at about day six following fertilization or cloning. At this stage, called the blastocyst stage (the stage just prior to the point of natural implantation in the womb), the embryo consists of a trophoblast (outer layer of cells which form the placenta) that surrounds the inner cell mass, which contains the pluripotent stem cells that have the potential to develop into any part of the human being.

The Humanistic View

After the embryo is destroyed and the stem cells have been harvested, these cells are grown in the laboratory. In theory, the cells can be induced to develop into any tissue needed to treat or cure a specific disease. However, the actual treatment of disease using embryonic stem cells is, as yet, a promise without much proof from the scientific community. Furthermore, even if embryonic stem cell research does produce treatments or cures, the term "therapeutic cloning" is nevertheless an oxymoron in that its practice would result not in therapeutic gain, but loss of life, for the embryos from whom such cells are derived. What should Christians think about "therapeutic" cloning, and how should they respond to such technological "advancements"? First, they must acquire an understanding of the worldview behind these new technologies. A basic humanistic, utilitarian worldview advocates choosing the course of action that promises to achieve the greatest amount of value. If one follows the language used in the debates on both cloning and embryonic stem cell research, the utilitarian worldview is very apparent. Robert Lanza, vice president of medical and scientific development at Advanced Cell Technology, stated in a news release which was later printed in the *Washington Post*, "Our intention is not to create cloned human beings, but rather to make life-saving therapies for a wide range of human disease conditions, including diabetes, strokes, cancer, AIDS, and neurodegenerative disorders such as Parkinson's and Alzheimer's disease."

> *"All life—even in its most innocent and earliest form— is a gift from God."*

Similarly, in his statement on embryonic stem cell research, Senator Orrin Hatch (R-Utah) said that, "Stem cell research facilitates life. . . . Abortion destroys life; this is about saving lives. . . . The most pro-life position would be to help people who suffer from these maladies. . . . Why shouldn't we use these cells to benefit mankind?" These are only two of the many examples of the pervasiveness of the utilitarian worldview among those who promote this research. As Christians, we must realize that people who believe that human beings evolved from animals and who do not have a personal relationship with God often base their positions on issues such as cloning in the desire to cure disease at almost any cost, the desire to obtain more knowledge, or the desire to be "first" in a particular scientific achievement. Unfortunately, they lack the understanding that all life—even in its most innocent and earliest form—is a gift from God, created in His image and designed to carry out His purposes.

What Christians Must Do

Second, I believe that Christians need to possess a fundamental understanding of how they are to interact with the world and how Scripture applies to these issues. In Matthew 5:13, we are called to be the "salt of the earth." As that salt, we cannot only be hungry for God's truth, but must also be willing to share that truth with a lost and dying world. In Matthew 10:16, when the disciples were sent to minister in the cities they were told to "be as shrewd as snakes and as innocent as doves." We need to follow this example and strive to be wise in our dealings with unbelievers, as well as to always "speak the truth in love" (Ephesians 4:16) to them. It is crucial that we realize that God is sovereign in these matters, that He allows all things for a purpose, and that only He can change people's hearts. However, this cannot be an excuse to ignore the current issues and refuse to speak out when necessary on these matters. Indeed, in Matthew 22:22, we are not called just to "love the Lord our God with all our hearts and souls" but also with our minds. The church for so long has lived in an "anti-intellectual" state of existence. However, Christians cannot go on thinking that bioethical issues will take care of themselves. We must begin grappling very seriously with these issues, or we will be taken by surprise and shock when our tax dollars begin being used to pay for atrocities that our post-modern society calls "technology."

Scripture teaches that all human life is created in God's image. Genesis 1:26–27 states "Then God said, 'Let us make man in our image, in our likeness.'. . . So God created man in his own image, in the image of God he created him; male and female he created them." The fact that human beings are created in God's image is repeated throughout Scripture and gives us our innate value. Our value, then, does not come from our contributions to society, as the humanistic worldview touts, but rather from our identity as creatures created in the image of our loving God. What does God say about the destruction of human life, all of which bears His image? Genesis 9:6 states "Whoever sheds the blood of man by man shall his blood be shed; for in the image of God has God made man." Here we can clearly see that the punishment for destroying human life is death, and the reason for this severe penalty is because that life was created in God's image. Finally, when looking at the life of the unborn, we cannot ignore Psalm 139:13–16, which states, "For you created my inmost being; you knit me together in my mother's womb. I praise you because I am fearfully and wonderfully made; your works are wonderful, I know that full well. My frame was not hidden from you when I was made in the secret place. When I was woven together in the depths of the earth, your eyes saw my unformed body. All the days ordained for me were written in your book before one of them came to be." As Christians, we know that embryos are living human beings who have innate value given by our awesome and sovereign God. In light of this, we can do no less than to stand against technologies that necessitate the destruction of embryonic human life.

Embryonic Stem Cell Research Destroys Human Lives

by E. Christian Brugger

About the author: *E. Christian Brugger is an assistant professor of ethics in the department of religious studies at Loyola University in New Orleans.*

Human development begins when the head of a *male gamete* (sperm cell) penetrates the cell wall of a *female gamete* (ovum or egg), the nuclei of the two cells fuse together, and the genetic material (DNA) from both cells—23 chromosomes each—combine. This process, which is called fertilization or conception, gives rise to an entirely new and genetically unique individual called a *zygote*. The zygotic individual contains all the genetic information and dynamism necessary to orchestrate its development from a zygote to an embryo, to a fetus, an infant, toddler, adolescent, and adult. The capacity of this single-celled human zygote to develop into an organically mature human person (i.e., the capacity for total human development) is termed *totipotency.*

The developmental process continues with the first cell division. In the hours after fertilization, the single-celled zygote divides into two identical cells, both of which are totipotent. The pair of cells divides again, producing four totipotent cells, and again, producing eight, and so on.

At approximately day five, the aggregate of totipotent cells begins to take the specialized form of a hollow sphere of cells, like a tiny basketball. The sphere has a layer of cells on the outside and a cluster of cells on the inside called the *inner cell mass* (picture a clump of attached marbles inside a basketball). The individual at this stage is called a *blastocyst.* The outer cell layer of the blastocyst will go on to form the placenta and other supporting tissues needed for fetal development in the uterus, while the cells of the inner cell mass—also called *stem cells*—will go on to form virtually all the organs and tissues of the human body.

Although the inner cell mass cells have the capacity to form virtually every type of cell in the human body (e.g., cardiac, neural, muscular, skeletal), they can no longer form a total organism because they are unable to give rise to the placenta and supporting tissues necessary for development in the uterus. So although they are not totipotent, each inner cell mass cell (i.e., each stem cell) is still *pluripotent* (i.e., while unable to develop into a complete organism, each cell has the potential to develop into the different tissue types in the human body).

In time these stem cells will undergo further specialization into *specialized* stem cells committed to specific kinds of tissue production (e.g., blood stem cells, cardiac stem cells, neural stem cells). Once a stem cell's code is "turned on," it is no longer pluripotent, but rather *multipotent* (i.e., has the capacity to generate a particular type of tissue).

Creating Embryos

Because of their wide-ranging capacities to produce human tissue types, both pluripotent and multipotent stem cells are coveted by clinical scientists, who see in them great potential for generating healthy tissue for persons who require the repairing or replacing of diseased or damaged tissue. These stem cells are extracted from human embryos in the blastocyst stage. There are two ways by which embryos can be created in a laboratory: *in vitro* fertilization (IVF) and cloning. IVF entails harvesting a female egg from a donor and fertilizing it in a petri dish using donor sperm. The resulting embryo is grown in a nutrient rich medium for four to seven days, at which point its inner cell mass cells (i.e., stem cells) are mature enough for harvesting.

The other method, cloning—the most common type called *somatic cell nuclear transfer*—involves harvesting an unfertilized female egg and carefully extracting its nucleus. The nuclear contents are then discarded, leaving the egg "enucleated." A somatic cell (i.e., any cell from the human body other than an egg or sperm cell) is then harvested from another donor, its nucleus likewise extracted, but rather than discarding its contents, the nuclear contents are transferred into the enucleated egg. Since an individual's virtually entire genetic blueprint is contained, in the form of DNA, in the nucleus of each somatic cell, the donor egg, after receiving the somatic cell's nucleus, now has a complete 46-chromosome genetic complement, all it would have if the egg had been fertilized by a male sperm cell. It needs only to begin dividing for the process of human development to proceed. Stimulate it with an electrical impulse or chemicals and, if successful, you get an actively dividing human embryo who is almost genetically identical, not with the woman who donated the egg, but with the donor of the somatic cell (who may be male or female). As with the IVF-made embryo, the cloned embryo would be cultivated in a laboratory and its stem cells matured and extracted. Embryo cloning for purposes of stem cell extraction is commonly called *therapeutic cloning*, a misnomer indeed, since the technique is manifestly un-therapeutic to the embryo. (The technique can also be used for making babies, commonly called *reproductive cloning*. In this case, the cloned embryo would be implanted into a female uterus and carried to term.)

If experimentation of this sort is welcomed by the Western world, then a massive for-profit industry will develop around these techniques. Huge numbers of human embryos will be created, frozen in cryo-labs (freezing labs), stored in embryo freezers, thawed, cultivated, harvested for stem cells, and then, when their utility has ceased, their useless remains will be destroyed and dumped.

The Human Status of Embryos

The crucial ethical question is this: What is the status of the human embryo? Is it *human life*, as prolife advocates and the Catholic Church affirm (see "Declaration on Use of Human Embryonic Stem Cells," Pontifical Academy for Life, Aug. 2000)? Or is it merely pre- or potential human life, as pro-embryo research advocates claim? If it is merely pre-human, then when we are dealing with the human embryo we are not dealing with a unique human being. Hence, lethal experimentation, which for compelling reasons—such as the development of life-saving medical procedures—could be justified, would not be the killing of human beings. But if the human embryo is human life and hence a human being, then this kind of experimentation would entail the wide-scale creation of human beings in the laboratory, their exploitation for purposes unrelated to their own welfare, and their ultimate destruction. It would be the creation, use, and killing of human beings—lots and lots of human beings. Defenders of stem cell research doubt whether the embryo is human life. To them the scientific and clinical benefits of embryo experimentation outweigh the presumption in favor of preserving what they argue is merely potential human life. They frequently place the question of the status of the embryo outside the domain of science, relegating it to the domains of philosophy or religion. Now, no one is doubting that philosophy and religion have something to say to the question, and even that people's ethical judgments are often shaped exclusively by their religious or philosophical views. But the question of the status of the human embryo is not exclusively or even primarily a philosophical or theological one. The question is first and foremost a matter for empirical observation.

> *"When we are dealing with a human embryo, we are dealing with a tiny human being."*

Before fertilization the egg and sperm cells are clearly not unique human individuals. Both are body cells of other human individuals, extensions we might say of those individuals, as an epithelial or epidermal cell is part of someone's body. *After* fertilization we are no longer dealing with a part of another's body, but an entirely new, genetically unique and organized individual. Unless seriously defective or prevented from the outside, this organism will develop into a completely differentiated fetus, which in due course will eventually be born, in the majority of instances alive and healthy. This organism is manifestly alive, that is, it has its own principle of unity and dynamism (though still in need of placental nurture) and it is manifestly human, that is, it is not the embryo of a frog, a mosquito, or a bat. Should we not therefore conclude it is human life? And doesn't conventional language as found among family and friends, ob-gyns, *What to Expect When You Are Expecting*, and dealers in baby apparel commonly refer to this human organism as a "baby," even as "he" or "she"? "Son, I'm worried that Carrie is having another baby; are you sure you can support another child?" "Congratulations, Sherry, have you found out yet whether it's a girl like granny hopes?" "Dr. Hortence, can you see from the ultrasound yet whether it's a boy or a girl?" Might not common parlance be telling us something?

But there is an even better reason for concluding that the human embryo is more than a blob of protoplasm, for there is no discreet point after the moment this new organism comes to be at which we can say, "*now* human life *is* present while *then* it was *not*," neither at the onset of differentiation, nor at the point of viability, nor at birth, toddlerhood, childhood, adolescence, or adulthood. Any attempt to draw a line after fertilization is arbitrary. Development from 40 minutes to 40 days to 40 years is a steady, organized continuum which will cease only if the organism itself ceases (i.e., dies). Everything the fetus has at 40 days or the man at 40 years is coded for and anticipated by the zygote in its first moments of existence. Therefore, drawing the line at the blastocyst stage is as arbitrary as drawing it at the first recognizable sign of neural tissue development, the beginning of a heartbeat, or at viability (which becomes earlier with better technology). Indeed, the only point at which something radically and entirely new begins or occurs is the point at which the organism becomes what it is, and that point is at *fertilization*. Compared to that, everything else is incidental development in size and form.

Like an oak tree is an acorn writ large, so a fully grown man or woman is an embryo writ large. One thing everyone reading this article can say with scientific certitude is, "I was an embryo." Had someone destroyed the embryonic life that you and I once were, is there any doubt he would have destroyed you and me? There was no point after you and I were conceived when you and I were not in a real substantive sense *you* and *me*. If, therefore, we look strictly at the empirical evidence, it is reasonable to conclude that when we are dealing with a human embryo, we are dealing with a tiny human being, and that destroying that embryo is destroying a human life.

No Moral Justification

Let's approach the ethical question from another angle. If you were hunting in a forest and saw at a distance something stirring in the bushes but were uncertain whether the stirring was that of a deer or another hunter, would you be morally justified in *shooting to kill* based simply on the premise that the figure you see stirring in the distance "might not" be another human? If it turned out to be another hunter and you shot and killed him, would the dead man's wife and fatherless children, or a jury of your peers, or Dan Rather and the CBS news team, or any reasonable person say that your decision to shoot was ethically warranted *based simply on the fact that you were unsure of the status of the object moving in the distance?* So even if we begin from the doubtful premise that the status of the embryo is uncertain (something empirical evidence, as I have shown, argues against), should we be willing to proceed with experimentation that results in the destruction of organisms which in the absence of better empirical evidence present themselves to us as living human beings? Unless we are *certain* that what we are dealing with is *not* a human being (and who could *truly* be certain?), then to proceed with experimentation of this kind says we are willing, even if wrong, to experiment on and kill innocent human beings. A will willing to kill the innocent is a bad will.

> *"Any deliberate action that destroys innocent human life at any stage from conception to natural death is wrong."*

But what about the great good that could result? Doesn't helping other people, perhaps large numbers of other people, overcome disease and suffering justify the destruction of embryos? Let's answer with another question. In attempting to balance out economic inequalities, were the Bolshevik revolutionaries justified in killing off the aristocracy and real or suspected political opponents? Because a goal is good, it doesn't mean all ways of pursuing that goal are good. A good end does not justify an evil means (see Rom. 3:8). Sound moral reasoning confirms that any deliberate action that destroys innocent human life at any stage from conception to natural death is wrong. The fact that an embryo is small and we are large is insufficient ground for concluding that the former can be destroyed. In fact, the opposite is the case; precisely because the human embryo is voiceless and defenseless, and can't fight back, all good people, especially Christians, must speak out and fight on behalf of innocent and helpless human life.

The humanity of the human embryo is not a religious question, but a matter of empirical fact. What is at stake at present is the production of tiny human lives for reasons entirely unrelated to the good of those lives. A new watershed is about to be crossed in our nation no less momentous than the one crossed in 1973 when the Supreme Court invented the constitutional right of abortion. And given the fact that there are morally acceptable alternative sources for stem cells—for example, stem cells found in adult bone marrow, adipose tissue, fetal umbilical cords and placenta, which, according to the latest research, promise equal if not greater results than embryonic stem cells—the question of proceeding with the making and destroying of human embryos should not even be an issue. After the grave mistakes and horrors of the past century, shouldn't we resist the temptation to watch silently while an entire class of human beings, in this case embryonic human life, is resigned to a moral status no higher than a laboratory rat?

Adult Stem Cell Research Should Replace Embryonic Stem Cell Research

by Maureen L. Condic

About the author: *Maureen L. Condic is an assistant professor of neurobiology and anatomy at the University of Utah.*

In August [2001], President [George W.] Bush approved the use of federal funds to support research on a limited number of existing human embryonic stem cell lines. The decision met with notably mixed reactions. Proponents of embryonic stem cell research argue that restricting federal funding to a limited number of cell lines will hamper the progress of science, while those opposed insist that any use of cells derived from human embryos constitutes a significant breach of moral principles. It is clear that pressure to expand the limits established by the President will continue. It is equally clear that the ethical positions of those opposed to this research are unlikely to change.

Regrettably, much of the debate on this issue has taken place on emotional grounds, pitting the hope of curing heartrending medical conditions against the deeply held moral convictions of many Americans. Such arguments frequently ignore or mischaracterize the scientific facts. To arrive at an informed opinion on human embryonic stem cell research, it is important to have a clear understanding of precisely what embryonic stem cells are, whether embryonic stem cells are likely to be useful for medical treatments, and whether there are viable alternatives to the use of embryonic stem cells in scientific research.

A Fascinating Process

Embryonic development is one of the most fascinating of all biological processes. A newly fertilized egg faces the daunting challenge of not only generating all of the tissues of the mature animal but organizing them into a functionally integrated whole. Generating a wide range of adult cell types is not an ability unique to embryos. Certain types of tumors called teratomas are extraordinarily adept at generating adult tissues, but unlike embryos, they do so without the benefit of an organizing principle or blueprint. Such tumors rapidly produce skin, bone, muscle, and even hair and teeth, all massed together in a chaotic lump of tissue. Many of the signals required to induce formation of specialized adult cells must be present in these tumors, but unlike embryos, tumors generate adult cell types in a hopelessly undirected manner.

If a developing embryo is not to end up a mass of disorganized tissues, it must do more than generate adult cell types. Embryos must orchestrate and choreograph an elaborate stage production that gives rise to a functional organism. They must direct intricate cell movements that bring together populations of cells only to separate them again, mold and shape organs through the birth of some cells and the death of others, and build ever

> *"There are at least three compelling scientific arguments against the use of embryonic stem cells as a treatment for disease and injury."*

more elaborate interacting systems while destroying others that serve only transient, embryonic functions. Throughout the ceaseless building, moving, and remodeling of embryonic development, new cells with unique characteristics are constantly being generated and integrated into the overall structure of the developing embryo. Science has only the most rudimentary understanding of the nature of the blueprint that orders embryonic development. Yet, recent research has begun to illuminate both how specific adult cells are made as well as the central role of stem cells in this process.

The term "stem cell" is a general one for any cell that has the ability to divide, generating two progeny (or "daughter cells"), one of which is destined to become something new and one of which replaces the original stem cell. In this sense, the term "stem" identifies these cells as the source or origin of other, more specialized cells. There are many stem cell populations in the body at different stages of development. For example, all of the cells of the brain arise from a neural stem cell population in which each cell produces one brain cell and another copy of itself every time it divides. The very earliest stem cells, the immediate descendants of the fertilized egg, are termed embryonic stem cells, to distinguish them from populations that arise later and can be found in specific tissues (such as neural stem cells). These early embryonic stem cells give rise to all the tissues in the body, and are therefore considered "totipotent" or capable of generating all things.

While the existence of early embryonic stem cells has been appreciated for some time, the potential medical applications of these cells have only recently become apparent. More than a dozen years ago, scientists discovered that if the normal connections between the early cellular progeny of the fertilized egg were disrupted, the cells would fall apart into a single cell suspension that could be maintained in culture. These dissociated cells (or embryonic stem cell "lines") continue to divide indefinitely in culture. A single stem cell line can produce enormous numbers of cells very rapidly. For example, one small flask of cells that is maximally expanded will generate a quantity of stem cells roughly equivalent in weight to the entire human population of the earth in less than sixty days. Yet despite their rapid proliferation, embryonic stem cells in culture lose the coordinated activity that distinguishes embryonic development from the growth of a teratoma. In fact, these early embryonic cells in culture initially appeared to be quite unremarkable: a pool of identical, relatively uninteresting cells.

First impressions, however, can be deceiving. It was rapidly discovered that dissociated early embryonic cells retain the ability to generate an astounding number of mature cell types in culture if they are provided with appropriate molecular signals. Discovering the signals that induce the formation of specific cell types has been an arduous task that is still ongoing. Determining the precise nature of the cells generated from embryonic stem cells has turned out to be a matter of considerable debate. It is not at all clear, for example, whether a cell that expresses some of the characteristics of a normal brain cell in culture is indeed "normal"—that is, if it is fully functional and capable of integrating into the architecture of the brain without exhibiting any undesirable properties (such as malignant growth). Nonetheless, tremendous excitement accompanied the discovery of dissociated cells' generative power, because it was widely believed that cultured embryonic stem cells would retain their totipotency and could therefore be induced to generate all of the mature cell types in the body. The totipotency of cultured embryonic stem cells has not been demonstrated and would, in fact, be difficult to prove. Nonetheless, because it is reasonable to assume embryonic stem cells in culture retain the totipotency they exhibit in embryos, this belief is held by many as an article of faith until proven otherwise.

Arguments Against the Use of Embryonic Stem Cells

Much of the debate surrounding embryonic stem cells has centered on the ethical and moral questions raised by the use of human embryos in medical research. In contrast to the widely divergent public opinions regarding this research, it is largely assumed that from the perspective of science there is little or no debate on the matter. The scientific merit of stem cell research is most commonly characterized as "indisputable" and the support of the scientific community as "unanimous." Nothing could be further from the truth. While the scientific advantages and potential medical application of embryonic stem cells have received considerable attention in the public media, the equally compelling scientific and medical *disadvantages* of transplanting embryonic stem cells or their derivatives into patients have been ignored.

There are at least three compelling scientific arguments against the use of embryonic stem cells as a treatment for disease and injury. First and foremost, there are profound immunological issues associated with putting cells derived from one human being into the body of another. The same compromises and complications associated with organ transplant hold true for embryonic stem cells. The rejection of transplanted cells and tissues can be slowed to some extent by a good "match" of the donor to the patient, but except in cases of identical twins (a perfect match), transplanted cells will eventually be targeted by the immune system for destruction. Stem cell transplants, like organ transplants, would not buy you a "cure"; they would merely buy you time. In most cases, this time can only be purchased at the dire price of permanently suppressing the immune system.

The proposed solutions to the problem of immune rejection are either scientifically dubious, socially unacceptable, or both. Scientists have proposed large scale genetic engineering of embryonic stem cells to alter their immune characteristics and provide a better match for the patient. Such a manipulation would not be trivial; there is no current evidence that it can be accomplished at all, much less as a safe and routine procedure for every patient. The risk that genetic mutations would be introduced into embryonic stem cells by genetic engineering is quite real, and such mutations would be difficult to detect prior to transplant.

Alternatively, the use of "therapeutic cloning" has been proposed. In this scenario, the genetic information of the original stem cell would be replaced with that of the patient, producing an embryonic copy or "clone" of the patient. This human clone would then be grown as a source of stem cells for transplant. The best scientific information to date from animal cloning experiments indicates that such "therapeutic" clones are highly likely to be abnormal and would not give rise to healthy replacement tissue.

The final proposed resolution has been to generate a large bank of embryos for use in transplants. This would almost certainly involve the creation of human embryos with specific immune characteristics ("Wanted: sperm donor with AB+ blood type") to fill in the "holes" in our collection. Intentionally producing large numbers of human embryos solely for scientific and medical use is not an option most people would be willing to accept. The three proposed solutions to the immune problem are thus no solution at all.

Potential Disasters

The second scientific argument against the use of embryonic stem cells is based on what we know about embryology. In an opinion piece published in the *New York Times* ("The Alchemy of Stem Cell Research," July 15, 2001) a noted stem cell researcher, Dr. David Anderson, relates how a seemingly insignificant change in "a boring compound" that allows cells to stick to the petri dish proved to be critical for inducing stem cells to differentiate as neurons. There is good scientific reason to believe the experience Dr. Anderson describes is likely to be the norm rather than a frustrating exception. Many of the factors required for the correct differentiation of embryonic cells are not chemicals that can be readily "thrown into the bubbling cauldron of our petri dishes." Instead, they are structural or mechanical elements uniquely associated with the complex environment of the embryo.

Cells frequently require factors such as mechanical tension, large scale electric fields, or complex structural environments provided by their embryonic neighbors in order to activate appropriate genes and maintain normal gene-expression patterns. Fully reproducing these nonmolecular components of the embryonic environment in a petri dish is not within the current capability of experimental science, nor is it likely to be so in the near future. It is quite possible that even with "patience, dedication, and financing to support the work," we will never be able to replicate in a culture dish the nonmolecular factors required to get embryonic stem cells "to do what we want them to."

"The scientific, ethical, and political advantages of using adult stem cells instead of embryonic ones are significant."

Failing to replicate the full range of normal developmental signals is likely to have disastrous consequences. Providing some but not all of the factors required for embryonic stem cell differentiation could readily generate cells that appear to be normal (based on the limited knowledge scientists have of what constitutes a "normal cell type") but are in fact quite abnormal. Transplanting incompletely differentiated cells runs the serious risk of introducing cells with abnormal properties into patients. This is of particular concern in light of the enormous tumor-forming potential of embryonic stem cells. If only one out of a million transplanted cells somehow failed to receive the correct signals for differentiation, patients could be given a small number of fully undifferentiated embryonic stem cells as part of a therapeutic treatment. Even in very small numbers, embryonic stem cells produce teratomas, rapid growing and frequently lethal tumors. (Indeed, formation of such tumors in animals is one of the scientific assays for the "multipotency" of embryonic stem cells.) No currently available level of quality control would be sufficient to guarantee that we could prevent this very real and horrific possibility.

The final argument against using human embryonic stem cells for research is based on sound scientific practice: we simply do not have sufficient evidence from animal studies to warrant a move to human experimentation. While there is considerable debate over the moral and legal status of early human embryos, this debate in no way constitutes a justification to step outside the normative practice of science and medicine that requires convincing and reproducible evidence from animal models prior to initiating experiments on (or, in this case, with) human beings. While the "potential promise" of embryonic stem cell research has been widely touted, the data supporting that promise is largely nonexistent.

To date there is *no* evidence that cells generated from embryonic stem cells can be safely transplanted back into adult animals to restore the function of damaged or diseased adult tissues. The level of scientific rigor that is normally applied (indeed, legally required) in the development of potential medical treatments would have to be entirely ignored for experiments with human embryos to proceed. As our largely disappointing experience with gene therapy should remind us, many highly vaunted scientific techniques frequently fail to yield the promised results. Arbitrarily waiving the requirement for scientific evidence out of a naive faith in "promise" is neither good science nor a good use of public funds.

Adult Stem Cells Are a Better Option

Despite the serious limitations to the potential usefulness of embryonic stem cells, the argument in favor of this research would be considerably stronger if there were no viable alternatives. This, however, is decidedly not the case. [Since the late 1990s,] tremendous progress has been made in the field of adult stem cell research. Adult stem cells can be recovered by tissue biopsy from patients, grown in culture, and induced to differentiate into a wide range of mature cell types.

The scientific, ethical, and political advantages of using adult stem cells instead of embryonic ones are significant. Deriving cells from an adult patient's own tissues entirely circumvents the problem of immune rejection. Adult stem cells do not form teratomas. Therapeutic use of adult stem cells raises very few ethical issues and completely obviates the highly polarized and acrimonious political debate associated with the use of human embryos. The concern that cells derived from diseased patients may themselves be abnormal is largely unwarranted. Most human illnesses are caused by injury or by foreign agents (toxins, bacteria, viruses, etc.) that, if left untreated, would affect adult and embryonic stem cells equally. Even in the minority of cases where human illness is caused by genetic factors, the vast majority of such illnesses occur relatively late in the patient's life. The late onset of genetic diseases suggests such disorders would take years or even decades to reemerge in newly generated replacement cells.

In light of the compelling advantages of adult stem cells, what is the argument against their use? The first concern is a practical one: adult stem cells are more difficult than embryonic ones to grow in culture and may not be able to produce the very large numbers of cells required to treat large numbers of patients. This is a relatively trivial objection for at least two reasons. First, improving the proliferation rate of cells in culture is a technical problem that science is quite likely to solve in the future. Indeed, substantial progress has already been made towards increasing the rate of adult stem cell proliferation. Second, treating an individual patient using cells derived from his own tissue ("antologous transplant") would not require the

> *"There is no compelling scientific argument for the public support of research on human embryos."*

large numbers of cells needed to treat large populations of patients. A slower rate of cell proliferation is unlikely to prevent adult stem cells from generating sufficient replacement tissue for the treatment of a single patient.

The more serious concern is that scientists don't yet know how many mature cell types can be generated from a single adult stem cell population. Dr. Anderson notes, "Some experiments suggest these [adult] stem cells have the potential to make mid-career switches, given the right environment, but in most cases this is far from conclusive." This bothersome limitation is not unique to adult stem cells. Dr. Anderson goes on to illustrate that in most cases the evidence suggesting scientists can induce embryonic stem cells to follow a specific career path is equally far from conclusive. In theory, embryonic stem cells appear to be a more attractive option because they are clearly capable (in an embryonic environment) of generating all the tissues of the human body. In practice, however, it is extraordinarily difficult to get stem cells *of any age* "to do what you want them to" in culture.

The Promise of Adult Stem Cells

There are two important counterarguments to the assertion that the therapeutic potential of adult stem cells is less than that of embryonic stem cells because adult cells are "restricted" and therefore unable to generate the full range of mature cell types. First, it is not clear at this point whether adult stem cells *are* more restricted than their embryonic counterparts. It is important to bear in mind that the field of adult stem cell research is not nearly as advanced as the field of embryonic stem cell research. Scientists have been working on embryonic stem cells for more than a decade, whereas adult stem cells have only been described within the last few years. With few exceptions, adult stem cell research has demonstrated equal or greater promise than embryonic stem cell research at a comparable stage of investigation. Further research may very well prove that it is just as easy to teach an old dog new tricks as it is to train a willful puppy. This would not eliminate the very real problems associated with teaching *any* dog to do *anything* useful, but it would remove the justification for "age discrimination" in the realm of stem cells.

The second counterargument is even more fundamental. *Even if* adult stem cells are unable to generate the full spectrum of cell types found in the body, this very fact may turn out to be a strong scientific and medical advantage. The process of embryonic development is a continuous trade-off between potential and specialization. Embryonic stem cells have the potential to become anything, but are specialized at nothing. For an embryonic cell to specialize, it must make choices that progressively restrict what it can become. The greater the number of steps required to achieve specialization, the greater the scientific challenge it is to reproduce those steps in culture. Our current understanding of embryology is nowhere near advanced enough for scientists to know with confidence that we have gotten all the steps down correctly. If adult stem cells prove to have restricted rather than unlimited potential, this would indicate that adult stem cells have proceeded at least part way towards their final state, thereby reducing the number of steps scientists are required to replicate in culture. The fact that adult stem cell development has been directed by nature rather than by scientists greatly increases our confidence in the normalcy of the cells being generated.

There may well be multiple adult stem cell populations, each capable of forming a different subset of adult tissues, but no one population capable of forming everything. This limitation would make certain scientific enterprises considerably less convenient. However, such a restriction in "developmental potential" would not limit the *therapeutic potential* of adult stem cells for treatment of disease and injury. Patients rarely go to the doctor needing a full body replacement. If a patient with heart disease can be cured using adult cardiac stem cells, the fact that these "heart-restricted" stem cells do not generate kidneys is not a problem for the patient.

The field of stem cell research holds out considerable promise for the treatment of disease and injury, but this promise is not unlimited. There are real, possibly insurmountable, scientific challenges to the use of embryonic stem cells as a medical treatment for disease and injury. In contrast, adult stem cell research holds out nearly equal promise while circumventing the enormous social, ethical, and political issues raised by the use of human embryos for research. There is clearly much work that needs to be done before stem cells of any age can be used as a medical treatment. It seems only practical to put our resources into the approach that is most likely to be successful in the long run. In light of the serious problems associated with embryonic stem cells and the relatively unfettered promise of adult stem cells, there is no compelling scientific argument for the public support of research on human embryos.

Organizations to Contact

The editors have compiled the following list of organizations concerned with the issues presented in this book. The descriptions are derived from materials provided by the organizations. All have publications or information available for interested readers. The list was compiled on the date of publication of the present volume; the information provided here may change. Be aware that many organizations take several weeks or longer to respond to inquiries, so allow as much time as possible.

American Medical Association (AMA)
515 N. State St., Chicago, IL 60610
(800) 621-8335
Web site: www.ama-assn.org

AMA is the largest professional association for medical doctors. It helps set standards for medical education and practices, and it is a powerful lobby in Washington for physicians' interests. The association publishes journals for many medical fields, including the monthly *Archives of Surgery* and the weekly *JAMA*.

American Society for Reproductive Medicine (ASRM)
1209 Montgomery Hwy., Birmingham, AL 35216-2809
(205) 978-5000 • fax: (205) 978-5005
e-mail: asrm@asrm.org • Web site: www.asrm.org

Established in 1944, ASRM is a voluntary, nonprofit organization devoted to advancing knowledge and expertise in reproductive medicine and biology. Its members include obstetricians, gynecologists, nurses, and research scientists. The society publishes the journal *Fertility and Sterility*, the newsletters *ASRM News* and *Menopausal Medicine*, and booklets on reproductive medicine. The ASRM Ethics Committee issues policy statements on the responsible use of reproductive technologies.

American Society of Law, Medicine & Ethics (ASLME)
765 Commonwealth Ave., Suite 1634, Boston, MA 02215
(617) 262-4990 • fax: (617) 437-7596
e-mail: info@aslme.org • Web site: www.aslme.org

The ASLME aims to provide high-quality scholarship and debate to professionals in the fields of law, heath care, policy, and ethics. The society acts as a source of guidance and information through the publication of two quarterlies, the *Journal of Law, Medicine & Ethics* and the *American Journal of Law & Medicine*.

Campaign for Responsible Transplantation (CRT)
PO Box 2751, New York, NY 10163-2751
(212) 579-3477
e-mail: banxeno@yahoo.com • Web site: www.crt-online.org

CRT is a nonprofit organization that believes xenotransplantation (transplanting animal organs into humans) poses a grave threat to human health because of the risk of transferring deadly animal viruses to the human population. The goal of the organization is to ban xenotransplantation research. Publications available on the Web site include news updates and press releases.

Canadian Bioethics Society
561 Rocky Ridge Bay NW, Calgary, AL T3G 4E7 Canada
(403) 208-8027
e-mail: lmriddell@shaw.ca • Web site: www.bioethics.ca

The Canadian Bioethics Society is an organization composed of health care administrators, physicians, theologians, and other professionals concerned about medical ethics. The organization seeks to strengthen the links between people involved in health care and to unite them in a common cause. It also publishes a twice-yearly newsletter.

Center for Bioethics
University of Pennsylvania
3401 Market St. #320, Philadelphia, PA 19104
(215) 898-7136 • fax: (215) 573-3036
e-mail: webmaster@bioethics.upenn.edu • Web site: www.bioethics.upenn.edu

The Center for Bioethics at the University of Pennsylvania is the largest bioethics center in the world, and it runs the world's first and largest bioethics Web site. Faculty at the center conduct research on issues including human research and experimentation, genetic testing, and transplantation. Its newsletter *PennBioethics* is published twice each year.

Center for Bioethics and Human Dignity
2065 Half Day Rd., Bannockburn, IL 60015
(847) 317-8180 • fax: (847) 317-8101
e-mail: info@cbhd.org • Web site: www.cbhd.org

The Center for Bioethics and Human Dignity examines a variety of bioethical issues, including genetic engineering, stem cell research, and managed care. Its explorations also consider the contribution of biblical values to modern Western culture. Articles are available on the Web site.

Council for Responsible Genetics
5 Upland Rd., Suite 3, Cambridge, MA 02140
(617) 868-0870 • fax: (617) 491-5344
e-mail: crg@gene-watch.org • Web site: www.gene-watch.org

The council is a national organization of scientists, health professionals, trade unionists, women's health activists, and others who work to ensure that biotechnology is developed safely and in the public interest. The council publishes the bimonthly magazine *GeneWatch* and position papers. And published the book *Exploding the Gene Myth*.

Euthanasia Research and Guidance Organization (ERGO)
24829 Norris Ln., Junction City, OR 97448-9559
(541) 998-1873
e-mail: ergo@efn.org • Web site: www.finalexit.org

ERGO is a nonprofit educational organization that believes voluntary euthanasia and physician-assisted suicide can be ethical ways to end lives. The organization provides research on assisted dying. Essays and statistics are available on the Web site, and books can also be purchased there.

The Hastings Center
21 Malcolm Gordon Rd., Garrison, NY 10524-5555
(845) 424-4040 • fax: (845) 424-4545
e-mail: mail@thehastingscenter.org • Web site: www.thehastingscenter.org

The Hastings Center is an independent research institute that explores the medical, ethical, and social ramifications of biomedical advances. The center publishes books, papers, guidelines, and the bimonthly *Hastings Center Report.*

Kennedy Institute of Ethics
Healy, 4th Fl., Georgetown University, Washington, DC 20057
(202) 687-8099 • fax: (202) 687-8089
Web site: www.georgetown.edu/research/kie/site/index.htm

The institute sponsors research on medical ethics, including ethical issues surrounding the use of recombinant DNA and human gene therapy. It supplies the National Library of Medicine with an online database on bioethics and publishes an annual bibliography in addition to reports and articles on specific issues concerning medical ethics.

President's Council on Bioethics
1801 Pennsylvania Ave. NW, Suite 700, Washington, DC 20006
(202) 296-4669
e-mail: info@bioethics.gov • Web site: www.bioethics.gov

Founded in 2001, the President's Council on Bioethics advises the president on bioethical issues, explores the ethical impact of biomedical and scientific research, and offers a forum for the discussion of these issues. Publications by the council include the reports *Reproduction and Responsibility* and *Human Cloning and Human Dignity.*

United Network for Organ Sharing (UNOS)
P.O. Box 2484, Richmond, VA 23218
(804) 782-4800 • fax: (804) 782-4817
Web site: www.unos.org

UNOS is a system of transplant and organ procurement centers, tissue-typing labs, and transplant surgical teams. It was formed to help organ donors and people who need organs to find each other. By federal law, organs used for transplants must be cleared through UNOS. The network also formulates and implements national policies on equal access to organs and organ allocation, organ procurement, and AIDS testing. It publishes the monthly *UNOS Update.*

Web Sites

Euthanasia.com
e-mail: rsmithpl@hotmail.com • Web site: www.euthanasia.com

This Web site offers fact sheets on euthanasia, articles, and statements from the medical profession that support the contention that euthanasia and assisted suicide are wrong. Books and videos are also available for purchase.

Reproductive Technologies Web
e-mail: grhf@hsph.harvard.edu • Web site: www.hsph.harvard.edu/rt21/

Part of the Harvard School of Public Health Web site, the Reproductive Technologies Web offers articles and links on various aspects of reproductive technology. Topics covered on the site include contraceptive technologies and the relationship between race and reproductive technology.

Bibliography

Books

Michael C. Brannigan	*Ethical Issues in Human Cloning.* New York: Seven Bridges Press, 2001.
Arthur L. Caplan, James J. McCartney, and Dominic A. Sisti	*Health, Disease, and Illness: Concepts in Medicine.* Washington, DC: Georgetown University Press, 2004.
Audrey R. Chapman and Mark S. Frankel, eds.	*Designing Our Descendants: The Promises and Perils of Genetic Modifications.* Baltimore: Johns Hopkins University Press, 2003.
Richard J. Devine	*Good Care, Painful Choices: Medical Ethics for Ordinary People.* Mahwah, NJ: Paulist Press, 2004.
Paul Dolan and Jan Abel Olson	*Distributing Health Care: Economic and Ethical Issues.* Oxford, UK: Oxford University Press, 2002.
Kathleen Foley and Herbert Hendin, eds.	*The Case Against Assisted Suicide: For the Right to End-of-Life Care.* Baltimore: Johns Hopkins University Press, 2002.
Francis Fukuyama	*Our Posthuman Future: Consequences of the Biotechnology Revolution.* New York: Farrar, Straus, and Giroux, 2002.
D.J. Galton	*In Our Own Image: Eugenics and the Genetic Modification of People.* London: Little, Brown, 2001.
Suzanne Holland, Karen Lebacqz, and Laurie Zoloth, eds.	*The Human Stem Cell Debate: Science, Ethics, and Public Policy.* New York: Cambridge University Press, 2000.
Leon R. Kass	*Life, Liberty and the Defense of Dignity: The Challenge for Bioethics.* San Francisco: Encounter Books, 2002.
William Kristol and Eric Cohen, eds.	*The Future Is Now: America Confronts the New Genetics.* Lanham, MD: Rowman & Littlefield, 2002.
Paul Lauritzen, ed.	*Cloning and the Future of Human Embryo Research.* Oxford, UK: Oxford University Press, 2001.
Margaret Lock	*Twice Dead: Organ Transplants and the Reinvention of Death.* Berkeley: University of California Press, 2001.

Bibliography

Thomas A. Mappes and David DeGrazia, eds.   *Biomedical Ethics.* Boston: McGraw-Hill, 2001.

Glenn McGee   *The Perfect Baby: Parenthood in the New World of Cloning and Genetics.* Lanham, MD: Rowman & Littlefield, 2000.

Steven H. Miles   *The Hippocratic Oath and the Ethics of Medicine.* New York: Oxford University Press, 2004.

Ronald Munson   *Raising the Dead: Organ Transplants, Ethics, and Society.* New York: Oxford University Press, 2002.

Joseph Panno   *Stem Cell Research: Medical Applications and Ethical Controversy.* New York: Facts On File, 2004.

Gregory E. Pence   *Re-creating Medicine: Ethical Issues at the Frontiers of Medicine.* Lanham, MD: Rowman & Littlefield, 2000.

Michael Ruse and Christopher A. Pynes, eds.   *The Stem Cell Controversy: Debating the Issues.* Amherst, NY: Prometheus Books, 2003.

Sally Satel   *PC, M.D.: How Political Correctness Is Corrupting Medicine.* New York: Basic Books, 2000.

T. Wayne Shelton   *The Ethics of Organ Donation.* New York: Elsevier Science, 2001.

Wesley J. Smith   *Consumer's Guide to a Brave New World.* San Francisco: Encounter Books, 2004.

Wesley J. Smith   *Culture of Death: The Assault on Medical Ethics in America.* San Francisco: Encounter Books, 2000.

Gregory Stock   *Redesigning Humans: Our Inevitable Genetic Future.* Boston: Houghton Mifflin, 2002.

Robert M. Veatch   *Transplantation Ethics.* Washington, DC: Georgetown University Press, 2000.

Mary Warnock   *Making Babies: Is There a Right to Have Children?* Oxford, UK: Oxford University Press, 2002.

Ian Wilmut, Keith Campbell, and Colin Tudge   *The Second Creation: Dolly and the Age of Biological Control.* New York: Farrar, Straus, and Giroux, 2000.

Periodicals

Nell Boyce   "Down on the Organ Farm," *U.S. News & World Report*, June 16, 2003.

Larry R. Churchill   "We Are Our Genes—Not!" *World & I*, November 2001.

Jonathan Colvin   "Me, My Clone, and I (or in Defense of Human Cloning)," *Humanist*, May 2000.

Bobbie Farsides and Robert J. Dunlop   "Is There Such a Thing as a Life Not Worth Living?" *British Medical Journal*, June 16, 2002.

Cynthia Fox | "Why Stem Cells Will Transform Medicine," *Fortune*, June 11, 2001.

M.J. Friedrich | "Debating Pros and Cons of Stem Cell Research," *JAMA*, April 9, 2000.

Deal W. Hudson | "Stem Cells Equal Baby Parts," *Crisis*, May 2000.

Albert R. Jonsen | "Beating Up Bioethics," *Hastings Center Report*, September/October 2001.

David Masci | "'Designer' Humans," *CQ Researcher*, May 18, 2001.

Gilbert Meilaender | "Spare Embryos," *Weekly Standard*, August 26/September 2, 2002.

Michael J. Meyer and Lawrence J. Nelson | "Respecting What We Destroy," *Hastings Center Report*, January/February 2001.

Gautam Naik | "Therapeutic Cloning Holds Promise of Treating Disease," *Wall Street Journal*, April 27, 2001.

Amy Otchet | "Animal Transplants: Safe or Sorry?" *UNESCO Courier*, March 2000.

John J. Paris | "Harvesting Organs from Cadavers: An Ethical Challenge," *America*, April 29, 2002.

Mark Pickup | "The Murder of Tracy Latimer," *Human Life Review*, Spring 2001.

Paul Raeburn | "Human Tissue: Handle With Care," *BusinessWeek*, April 15, 2002.

Alejandro Reuss | "Cause of Death: Inequality," *Dollars and Sense*, May/June 2001.

Lawrence Rudden | "Death and the Law," *World & I*, May 2003.

Wesley J. Smith | "No Mercy in Florida," *Weekly Standard*, October 20, 2003.

Keith Taylor | "Was Dr. Kevorkian Right?" *Free Inquiry*, Spring 2003.

Robert Tracinski | "Attack of the Phantom Cloning Menace," *Intellectual Activist*, February 2003.

Prasad Venugopal | "Finding Cures or Fiddling with Nature?" *Political Affairs*, January 2002.

Nicholas Wade | "Grappling with the Ethics of Stem Cell Research," *New York Times*, July 24, 2001.

Caroline S. Wagner | "The Weapons of Mass Creation," *Los Angeles Times*, February 13, 2003.

Wall Street Journal | "The House Was Right to Ban Cloning," August 2, 2001.

Index

185